THE PROBLEM HOUSING ESTATE

To Sarah McCabe

The Problem Housing Estate

An Account of Omega and its People

FRANCES REYNOLDS

Gower

Published by
Gower Publishing Company Limited,
Gower House, Croft Road, Aldershot, Hants GU11 3HR,
England

and

Gower Publishing Company,
Old Post Road, Brookfield, Vermont 05036,
USA

British Library Cataloguing in Publication Data

Reynolds, Frances
   The problem housing estate : an account of
   Omega and its people.
   1. public housing——England——Midlands
   2. Midlands (England)——Social conditions
   I. Title
   942.4'085'8   HD7334.M/

   ISBN 0-566-05008-0

#13361336

Printed in Great Britain

Contents

Tables

Acknowledgements

The research reported here was carried out while I was Research Fellow at the Centre for Criminological Research, University of Oxford, where I received invaluable support and encouragement. I should like to express gratitude to the Joseph Rowntree Memorial Trust for funding the project and for their help and advice throughout. Alice Coleman of King's College London was an inspiring colleague to whom I am indebted for many of the ideas put forward in this report. Getting to know the people of Omega would not have been possible without the commitment and willingness to work antisocial hours of my two staunch Research Associates Frances Duffy and Phil Harding to whom many thanks. Thanks are also due to the many helpful people in the social services, the probation service, the police, the courts and the housing department in the local authority within which we worked, for permitting access to their records; and to the councillors, neighbourhood officers, community workers and other 'characters' on Omega who provided information and friendly interest. Above all it was the people of Omega who made the project possible, giving their time to answering our questions and dispensing innumerable cups of tea. I like to think that they enjoyed talking as much as we enjoyed listening. Finally my grateful thanks to Jenny Sumner and Terry Hastings who painstakingly and uncomplainingly produced the copy for publication.

1 Problem housing estates: a review of studies made and theories presented

Slum clearance did not eradicate concentrations of relative material deprivation, delinquency and other social problems. Indeed some council housing estates seem to have more problems than the rundown city areas used to, or do now, in that they are more likely to call for intervention and the input of resources. Sociological interest has focussed for many years now on 'problem' estates and it is worth charting briefly the way this interest came about.

The Chicago school of urban ecology (e.g. Shaw and McKay, 1942) saw the natural habitat of deviant lifestyles in the transitional zones of deteriorating property ringing the city commercial centre; the correlates were low rents and overcrowded dwellings, presence of immigrant minorities, a changing population, all of which contributed to what they believed to be the causal factor, social disorganisation leading to lack of community cohesion. The remedy was to stimulate democratic organisations of residents and set objectives for communal action schemes. This was subsequently tried in American ghettoes with government support during the 1960s, and in the 1970s with the Home Office funded Community Development Projects in deprived inner city areas of Britain (Lees and Smith, 1975). No longterm improvements in conditions resulted and support was withdrawn.

1

Areal studies became popular in Britain in the postwar period and with the massive redevelopment of that era there was, as Morris (1958) wrote:

> a shift of interest from the natural area which has grown up of its own accord to the 'planned' area which has resulted from conscious social and political deliberation.

Those researchers interested in plotting delinquency rates began to find that the council estates had as high or higher rates than the older urban areas. Mannheim (1948) found this to be the case in Cambridge; Ferguson (1952) found the same for Glasgow. Bagot (1941) had looked at some prewar estates in Liverpool and found a more promising picture which suggested that while delinquency was high on council housing estates at first, children born into the better conditions grew up to be more law-abiding. The implication was that the ex-slum dwellers brought their lifestyles with them.

Most British workers of the 1950s and 1960s were keen to attribute the continuing problems to learned subcultural norms rather than to family pathology. Morris for example in his study of Croyden (1958) found the highest concentrations of delinquents living on the prewar housing estates but, within the estates, delinquency correlated very significantly with being in the lowest social class and was localised in pockets in the least desirable back streets. Morris was probably the first researcher to suggest that housing allocation policies might have an unacknowledged role in forming 'rough' or 'respectable' areas. The lifestyle of the roughs he saw as being a pattern adapted in their previous conditions to low economic status and frequent stress situations. Jones (1958) comparing two same age housing estates with very different levels of delinquency concluded that the higher rate of tenant turnover on the bad estate accounted for its difficulties, a conclusion in line with the social disorganisation hypothesis of the Chicago school. The 'settled' estate in contrast:

> was becoming a community and beginning to develop and enforce community norms of behaviour.

Jones however failed to account for why the other estate had such a mobile population except to comment that one factor contributing to the lack of community controls was the:

> continuous flow of residents of low calibre from the slums.

Nevertheless, although findings varied and interpretations differed, the postwar criminologists generally anticipated that high delinquency rates on council estates would decline when the estates settled down and became communities. Mays for example could say with fair confidence in 1963 that while delinquency was:

> part of a general pattern of life which is carried over by the immigrants when they move to their new localities,

nevertheless:

> after the lapse of a generation or more delinquency rates fall and there is a general improvement in behaviour.

The idea of settling was also expressed in the wave of studies being done over the same period not concerned with delinquency but rather with the structures and relationships involved in making up a community. Again the impetus may well have come from the enthusiastic postwar planning destroying, with the best intentions, inner city neighbourhoods which over the generations had established colourful characters of their own. Some of these survived for a while. Kerr (1958) reported on the focal role of Mum in Ship Street; Young and Willmott (1957) told about the importance of the extended family networks in Bethnal Green which performed both a supportive and controlling function; in similar vein Mogey (1956) emphasised the self reliance, stability and friendliness of St. Ebbes. These last two studies followed some families from the old communities to the new council estates built for them. The message was the same from Greenleigh and from Barton that the effect of the move to the estates was to turn the nuclear family in upon itself so that members had to rely on each other for emotional support. Women, particularly, felt isolated and threatened by unfamiliar neighbours. The television replaced family visiting as entertainment and an increasing value was put on the acquisition of consumer goods. The problems of isolation and malaise that arose on these estates, confirmed by other authors such as Maule (1956), Morris and Mogey (1965), Mitchell et al. (1954), were again presumed to be temporary; means had to be found to promote the forging of bonds and relationships to replace the lost family network. The solutions proposed included the provision of community centres, playgrounds and shops and services; the organising of residents' associations to lobby councils to run social functions; and raising awareness among the medical and social services of the special support needed by dislocated families adapting to a strange

3

environment.

   Although those early studies were generally optimistic one problem, accurately diagnosed, was the divisions which emerged between different types of residents and the conflicts thus generated. As Kuper (1953) quoted a resident on a Coventry housing estate as saying:

> You can blueprint for houses but not for living together.

Thus in his study of neighbour relations he distinguished between the 'reserved' and the 'sociable' types between whom conflict was precipitated. Mitchell et al. (1954) working in the Sheffield and Liverpool estates noted the resentment between the 'roughs' and the 'respectables' and found that setting up a programme of activities at the community centre designed to establish neighbourly feelings but, inevitably, run mainly by respectables, only intensified the divisions. Morris and Mogey (1965) on the other hand did not find this situation because Berinsfield was occupied in the early days by families who had already squatted there in huts for years during the war and who knew each other. They commented on the subject of settling new estates in general:

> It seems unreasonable that clearance families should be expected to face simultaneous changes of home, neighbours and residential community.

Yet that is what usually happened with slum clearance and certainly could not be avoided on the newer estates which took families from the housing waiting list on the basis of accumulated points. On the other hand Mitchell et al. (1954) appeared to believe in getting the mixture right and proposed that:

> careful attention should be paid by housing authorities to the allocation of the houses to a sufficient variety of people who can be regarded as the raw material of a new community.

Kuper, whose study led him to believe that the reserved and the sociable types needed to live in differently planned neighbourhood units, suggested that applicants on the housing list might be involved in the planning stage of the houses and layouts of their future estates. The feeling was however very much one that new estates might produce problems inherent in the settling in process but these could be solved if the planning was right. Wilson's (1963) penetrating analysis of what it could mean to move to a new housing estate and how such areas could become 'difficult' was perhaps the first to emphasise the enormous

4

responsibility of the local authority in allocation, in providing amenities, in putting resources into community organisation, in making general practitioners aware of their social service role, and in providing specialist support for the minority of families for whom the stress was too much.

Unfortunately by the 1970s it was clear that the difficulties of housing estates did not always go away after people had settled in and amenities had been provided; that in many of them but by no means all, the same problems of delinquency, lack of care for the houses, family problems, neighbour problems, isolation and apathy, remained or increased. From a number of different quarters interest and concern was aroused. Criminologists Baldwin and Bottoms (1976) re-examined the:

> specifically urban and areal dimensions of the
> social processes that are connected with crime.

They felt that the wider perspective had been too long overlooked. Plotting areas of offender residence for the conurbation of Sheffield, Baldwin and Bottoms found the highest rate of juvenile delinquents came from council housing whereas the private rented areas had the highest adult offender rate. By 1981, after further demolition in the inner city areas, Bottoms and Xanthos found that:

> the council sector became easily the largest high
> offender rate type of tenure within the city.

The most striking finding of the study of Sheffield was the vast difference in offender rates between twenty four estates, the highest of which had rates twenty times that of the lowest. Nor did the rates vary with age of the estate; separating those built in the 1920s, 1930s, 1950s and 1960s, each group had estates with very high, and others with very low, delinquency rates refuting the 'time to settle' explanations. Bottoms and Xanthos looked at the case histories of three of the worst estates (in terms of delinquency rate and reputation) and argued that a combination of factors had been at work over time. Chief among them was the reputed character of the earliest settlers, in one case some notorious gang leaders from slum clearance; in another the first inhabitants were all high priority young families; in another case after a generation of respectability the chance arrival of some problem families altered the perceived tone of the district. Thereafter the second chief factor took over which was the consequence, unintended for the most part, of housing allocation policies and tenant choice including the initiation of transfers and exchanges out of the unpopular estates. The reverse process could be charted on one of the popular estates where the original settlers came as a group from a stable working class area, established a neighbourly and cohesive community, and the estate had since continued to be sought after, one to which respectable families wanted to move. Baldwin and Xanthos also gave weight to additional factors such as the possible existence of a deviant subculture on the older high delinquency rate estates which could account for the perpetuating of delinquency into successive generations; and the constraints on low status families, in terms of lack of choice, which forced them to take the first offer of a tenancy on the least desirable estates because they were desperate for housing.

At about the same time as the Sheffield study, Herbert, with his colleague Evans, was working from an urban geographer's point of view on a similar mapping of the delinquency areas of Cardiff. His overall conclusions were contained in Herbert (1982). Their work too found disparities in delinquency rates between estates of comparable age and social composition and showed that perceptions of these differences were recognised by residents on the estates and people elsewhere. For example one of the bad estates, Ely, was stigmatised from the beginning due to the characteristics of the first settlers, slum clearance tenants from a Catholic inner city area notorious for violence. Evans (1980) also collected evidence that parents in high delinquency areas were more tolerant of or ignored delinquent acts and more said they were ready to use physical punishment or call in the police or school if they had behaviour problems with a child. Herbert wrote from a structuralist standpoint to explain the continuing existence of areas of delinquency, relative material deprivation and other indicators of social malaise in terms of resource allocation in a competitive social and economic system which expresses itself in a spatial dimension.

This conceptual framework has great force and has been broadly accepted in this report but does not provide a full explanation, at least without further analysis, of all problem estates. It must not be taken for granted that estates with the highest rates of delinquency or agency intervention are always the ones with the greatest concentrations of material deprivation. While it is possible to make significant correlations of such measures with socioeconomic grouping, observation alone indicates that there can be areas such as mobile home parks or homogeneous concentrations of people such as Asian

6

immigrants which manifest poverty and substandard living conditions without developing a high rate of crime or a continual demand for social first aid. Baldwin and Bottoms (1976) found that holding social class and age of housing constant there were still big differences between estates.

While there is no evidence to support the idea that problem estates arise due to the numbers of pathologically inadequate families it would be naive to ignore the fact that some families cope less well and show less consideration for their neighbours than others, a situation which provokes trouble. Means (1977) for example in his study of an area of Birmingham scheduled for redevelopment, used by the corporation for the temporary dumping of problem families, found that the longstanding respectable residents of the streets involved had barraged the councillors with complaints about the behaviour of the imported roughs. A 'moral panic' was started by some councillors and exaggerated by the local press. Means interpreted the deviant lifestyle of some of the roughs as 'the only adaptive way of coping' with low economic status and continual stress, but acknowledged that they 'caused genuine upset and dismay amongst established residents'. Alcoholism, wife-battering, child neglect, misuse of the sanitation and constant vandalism by the children were examples. Means believed that the allocation policy and the media scare campaign had produced a situation of hostility or 'intra-class enmity' between the respectables and the roughs which was the expression of competition for scarce resources in the housing and social work markets.

Means' work would suggest that identifiable differences between types of resident and the spiralling effects of reputation are factors to be reckoned with in producing a problem area or estate. A number of studies have argued that reputation is the main causal factor, in that the deviant label itself 'amplifies' both the actual antisocial behaviour of residents and the recording of this by external agencies. In Armstrong and Wilson's case history of Easterhouse (1973) in Glasgow, it seemed that one estate out of several was picked out by the council as a lawless gang land needing positive intervention and a policy of increased police activity in that area escalated the violence. Local party politicians backed by the sensationalist press began to use the terrible example of Easterhouse in their battle for popular support for their policies. The authors believed that labelling the estate amplified the deviance by providing an image that had to be lived up to.

7

Another example is Gill's (1977) observational account of Luke Street, a rundown estate in Liverpool. Luke Street did not get off to a bad start. It was highly desirable before the war but with the building of large new estates of more modern council housing which required higher rents, it became a dumping ground for the housing department to place large low income families with low housekeeping standards. The resultant problems of high child density on the streets, the resentment of the older residents, and particularly the consequences of being officially low status and troublesome, 'created', according to Gill, a deviant subculture of crime and violence. Gill implied that police surveillance escalated the process producing anti-police attitudes. A restudy of the area by Gill's colleague Davies (1978) cast doubt on this interpretation. He interviewed 182 residents and found the majority took a very uncompromising view towards delinquents. They held parents to be responsible and recommended the birch as the best treatment. Eighty six per cent wanted more not less police in the area. It rather suggested that Gill, in seeing the delinquent subculture where he expected to see it, was more vulnerable to the effects of the labelling of Luke Street than the majority of residents whose reaction was fiercely that of the need to uphold law and order and the right of the respectable citizen to protection.

Damer (1976) tells the story of 'Wine Alley' a housing estate built in the 1930s in a working class area of Glasgow suffering from the depression. The locals expected to get the nice new houses and when it was discovered they were to go to slum clearance tenants from the Gorbals they were outraged. The initial situation was thus similar to that of Ely as described by Herbert (1982). This local resentment was reflected in the attitudes of corporation housing officials and the readiness of the press to sensationalise any misdemeanours of the new residents. Things got worse after the war when, according to the older residents of Wine Alley, 'riff-raff' were dumped in the houses and the estate became dilapidated and vandalised. Damer realised that Wine Alley residents had come to accept the deviant image of the estate as it was in the view of outsiders. However he argued that this internalised image did not create deviancy in the residents, it caused them to look for scapegoats to blame. Respectables blamed the 'riff-raff' and:

> locals retreat into the womb of their houses whence they view the outside world of their neighbours with fear and suspicion.

The role of the police in creating delinquency areas through differential policing caused by the reputation or label attached to a particular area has been challenged by Mawby (1979). He set out in the Sheffield study referred to above, to demonstrate that the effects of labelling explained the wide discrepancies in offender rates between comparable housing estates. Mawby found however that not only did the police have rather vague pictures of the crime rates and types of crimes typical of various residential areas, they were not aware of the striking differences in offender rates between otherwise similar estates. Moreover the discovery and recording of a crime was so heavily dependent upon victim or witness reporting that it became clear that the high recorded crime rates of the bad areas were a consequence of the high rate of complainants from those areas.

Thus to summarise briefly on the basis of the studies discussed so far, it seems that there is no evidence that public labelling was the cause of deviancy in a problem area; doubt is also cast on the subcultural theory of causation since most of the areas studied provided evidence of divisions and hostilities rather than a shared set of neighbourhood values or attitudes. The presence of rough antisocial families resented by established respectable residents was a common factor somewhere in the development of the bad reputation of problem estates wherever studied. In fact the evidence suggests that conflict between sections of the residential population (frequently demonstrated by a high rate of call-out and complaints to police) was the mark of the problem estate rather than economic deprivation as such. A high tenant turnover rate resulting from an estate's unpopularity could only make matters worse by increasing the polarisation of roughs and respectables both within and between estates.

A less analytical and more empirical approach to problem estates places the emphasis firmly on features of the planned environment and on the responsibilities of local authorities. This movement has been linked to a policy for action. The instigating force was Newman's book on 'Defensible Space' in 1972. Newman drew attention to the fact that much modern housing development contained large areas of unfenced surround, of stairways, of corridors and entrance halls which did not belong to anybody. Not only therefore did they remain uncared for, but they often became gathering points for young persons whose activities could not be subjected to surveillance. In other words some housing layouts positively attracted delinquents and provided inviting opportunities for such crimes as mugging and vandalism. Other kinds of social problems too could be precipitated by design features, such as the isolation and depression felt by young mothers in high rise flats and the stress caused by noise due to lack of insulation. A number of experimental projects were set up following the impact of Newman's ideas in the USA and in Britain which focussed on the prevention of the most visible measure of the problem estate, vandalism. Caretakers, entry-phones to blocks of flats, fenced areas round flats and maisonettes, laminated glass in stairway windows, graffiti-proof walls, brightly lit streets and doorways and a general improvement in the external appearance by planting trees and shrubs, all have met with varying degrees of success (see Wilson et al., 1978; Hunter, 1978; Mayhew, 1979; Power, 1981, 1982, 1984; Coleman, 1985).

A lesson that was learned from some of the earlier experiments was that improvements imposed by the authorities met with little cooperation; more important was that any environmental alterations must be the outcome of consultation with the tenants. Consultation too was emphasised in influential reports from Hedges et al. (1980) and from the Department of the Environment's Priority Estates Project (Power 1981, 1982, 1984) which concentrated on the importance of local authority administration of services in revitalising problem estates. In two of the studies referred to, the tenants of unpopular, fear-ridden and vandalised estates, Cunningham Road in Widnes and Tulse Hill in Brixton, were consulted. They declared their top priority was expediting repairs to the insides of their houses. Other complaints were lack of security, noisy neighbours, fast traffic, lack of playspace, rubbish dumping, delays in housepainting and other aspects of the external environment. It was plain that the drawn out process of getting necessary repairs done to the house interiors was the root of a lot of tenant frustration. The project team liaised with council officials who began to realise that their administrative structure and procedures were not comprehensible to tenants and not efficient when seen from the service delivery end. Four different departments were responsible for repairs and maintenance on the estate and, as Hedges et al. found, from the tenants' point of view:

Nobody seemed in charge; nobody seemed responsible; nobody seemed able to make a decision. Complaints and repair requests and the like were always passing between one department and another.

The answer in each of the two projects to this main problem was to reorganise the housing department on an area basis so that one manager became responsible for dealing with requests from the estate, and seeing they were put into operation. In Tulse Hill an estate office was opened which dealt with lettings and recorded complaints about repairs. In each case, with evidence of genuine concern by the authorities, tenants' representatives were elected with the specific objective of opening up permanent lines of communication with the authorities. Play areas, road humps to slow the traffic, the painting of the house exteriors allowing individual choice of colours and improved street lighting were among the improvements asked for by residents and acted upon by the council; a beat policeman began to patrol the estates and contributed to a greater feeling of security and better public relations.

One answer to increasing satisfaction on problem estates therefore could be administrative decentralisation. Ann Power (1981) wrote:

> Experience has shown just how hostile the public is to a remote town hall.

Instead, there should be:

> intensive estate-based management. The residents are in the front line . . . . but they must have some sense of being able to control the housing management effort.

The lessons of Cunningham Road were the same. Hedges et al. (1980) made an interesting point in their conclusions:

> People often say that the problem with consultation is that it raises people's expectations. But raising people's expectations is precisely what we need to do in this context because they will only take part if their expectations are raised.

This is a very significant comment. The councils responsible had expected to be requested to pay out a vast amount of capital in providing facilities; in fact it turned out on both estates that putting accessible human beings in a position to deliver efficiently services to which residents already had a right was the biggest single morale boosting innovation. Raising people's expectations that their rights to efficient services from their council landlords, or to have a say in the improving of their environment, would be honoured, raised the corporate self respect of the estates. Both estates developed a more desirable image and reputation which seemed to cause a

11

decrease in vandalism and dilapidation.

Interest in the role of housing management policies in preventing or causing, in fostering or improving, problem estates has also come in recent years from other sources including some local authorities. A high degree of consensus that a decentralisation of services and an increase in the responsibility of housing departments for the welfare of tenants has emerged from many different studies and approaches by such as the Centre for Environmental Studies (Popplestone and Paris, 1979), the Housing Research Group (1981) and Hadley and Hatch (1981) who applied the same formula to social services' organisation as well.

And during the same period there has been a parallel and growing realisation that policing methods in problem areas whether inner city slums or difficult housing estates are a significant factor. As with housing the recommendations coming from academics, government committees or policemen themselves (Alderson, 1977; Moore and Brown, 1981) have been for the police to develop bases in and relationships within each community.

In a structuralist context increasing public resources to particular areas in this way can only be viewed as tinkering with a system in which it is inevitable there will be losers somewhere at the bottom. However, as was stated earlier, problem estates are not definable simply in terms of economic deprivation. And if local authorities can learn to avoid, or take steps to compensate for, features of the environment or of administration which precipitate or foster social problems, then everyone will gain.

Indeed in many areas of the country in the early 1980s projects were set up by, or in cooperation with, local authorities to improve conditions on council estates on the basis of the convergent findings mentioned above. The case of Walsall (Seabrook, 1984) has now become a legend. During a brief spell of left wing Labour control from 1980 to 1982 thirty three neighbourhood offices were opened on the estates of Walsall, dealing with all housing matters such as rent, rates, repairs, transfers and lettings; giving welfare benefits advice; acting as a base for the home help and meals on wheels service; providing a referral service to other agencies. Groups and organisations were able to hold meetings on the premises. It was intended that the offices should be a base for social workers, community policemen, health visitors and educational welfare officers, but plans

12

were curtailed when power shifted in the town hall. In two years however the improved efficiency and accessibility of services to the estates in Walsall increased the morale and involvement of residents and the estate with the worst reputation was transformed.

Estate management and service delivery however cannot redress massive social injustice and some of the more recent attempts to rehabilitate severely disadvantaged and deteriorating estates such as the NACRO Safe Neighbourhoods project (Bright and Petterson, 1984) and the CES (1984) report on 'outer' estates in the north are less promising. Unless the political and economic climate changes it seems that these estates' continued decline into areas of 'subsistence' living is inevitable.

To recapitulate, over the years from the 1940s to the 1980s, there has been a change in attitude towards problem housing estates from one of sociological analysis through descriptive anthropology via urban geography to an emphasis on the role and the responsibility of the authorities and agencies which provide services and control and manage tenants' lives and thence ultimately to the system of resource allocation. The research to be presented in subsequent chapters draws from all of these precedents particularly in trying to construct explanatory concepts. But its inspiration came from the last category in viewing problem estates as the outcome of the decisions and mistakes of urban planning and local authority agencies for services and social control, and in looking to them for remedies.

The research work took place in 1981 to 1983 and focussed on one particular problem housing estate in a Midlands city. Everybody in the city including the residents of the estate knew it was a problem estate. But what made it a problem estate? Did people living there have more problems than other citizens or did the estate itself present a problem in some other way? Was it perhaps no worse than anywhere else but provided a scapegoat for the rest of the city? Was its awful image manufactured? If it really was worse than other places then how had this come about since there were other estates built at the same period in much the same style and which had taken tenants from the same housing waiting list as Omega?

The research therefore had three objectives: to discover whether according to objective measures Omega estate had more problems than other similar estates; to find out something of the activities, the experiences and the views of residents living on the estate by talking to them; and to draw conclusions from the findings which might have general applicability on what makes a problem estate.

The researchers interviewed by appointment the members of a random sample of over one hundred households on Omega estate. Where the family contained teenage children these were subsequently interviewed separately from their parents. The interviews took between one and two hours on average and covered topics which could be regarded as factual such as length of time in dwelling, condition of dwelling, membership of clubs, use of shops and buses and community centre and other amenities, contact with housing, social services, police and other agencies and experience of victimisation. Much of the material gathered was more subjective such as residents' opinions of the estate, of the neighbours, of councillors, social workers, policemen, schools, the all important housing department and what respondents' problems were and how they accounted for them. Interviewers were as informal as possible and although care was taken always to include open-ended questions on a list of specific issues, spontaneous contributions on any aspect of estate life were encouraged. In addition to the sample of residents all proprietors or managers of shops, take-aways, public houses and other commercial premises were interviewed as were local figures, persons holding posts in the community association, councillors, church people, teachers and professionals such as social workers involved on the estate. For a period of two years the researchers followed events and issues in estate life and began to feel identified with Omega and its problems.

The following chapters are an attempt to describe aspects of life on Omega which relate to its problem status as perceived by its inhabitants.

2 Omega estate: history and reputation

The headline of a local newspaper screamed 'Reign of terror at flats'. The 'exclusive' article went on to identify a particular block of flats on Omega estate. It claimed children were 'running riot' and threatening and terrorising residents. The report was written following a half term week and in the small print just four specific incidents were mentioned: a group of children hanging round on the stairs sniffing glue; a broken window; a door damaged by kicking; and a piece of burning cardboard pushed through a letter box. All these were unpleasant and perhaps frightening incidents from the viewpoint of the residents in the flats but no doubt similar acts were repeated in other areas of the city by bored children on half term holiday, shut out of their houses by parents at work and shouted at by annoyed tenants in the flats where they congregated. It may be that the only persons to telephone the police or the newspapers about the harassment came from Omega. Whatever the source only Omega got the shock-horror headlines, which reinforced yet again the bad image of the estate in the minds of residents and outsiders alike.

This image had been with Omega from the very beginning. The estate had been planned and built to cater for a massive postwar population overspill mainly caused by an increase in the demand for labour in the factories and works on the industrial side of the city. The rest of the city had always distanced itself from the drab dirty industrial area and the stigmatisation was increased by the largescale immigration of 'foreign' labour from Scotland, Ireland, Wales and elsewhere.

In addition, although slum clearance had been virtually completed by the late fifties when Omega estate was started, there was a widespread belief among city residents that people from the inner city slum clearance areas had been placed on Omega estate. Some of the early tenants on the estate also thought the same. One was quoted in the early days as saying:

> I don't like it up here getting all the tail end. It's a disgusting place. Putting all the backend up here won't give people like us a chance to make this a decent place to live.

Thus owing to its early associations with immigrant labour and with the last few slum clearance families Omega estate had a bad reputation from the beginning with the rest of the city. As a resident interviewed in this research commented:

> This estate carried a stigma from before it was built.

The planning decision was to use 250 acres of farmland on the edge of the city for one large 'properly planned community' which would be a 'final solution' to the city housing needs of the late fifties. Eventually the estate contained nearly three thousand houses and flats and provided shops, a community centre, a church, three primary schools, a secondary school, large playing fields and two recreation grounds and many other facilities. Such a development was very identifiable and did not merge easily into the rest of the city. The estate was built for families with children which made sense of a sort at the time since it was inevitable that the majority of applicants on the waiting list were in this category. In the fifties and sixties single persons or single parents could not register and since allocation depended on points, a young couple who registered on marriage were likely to have one or more babies by the time a tenancy came up.

Families moved in long before the roads or the shops or the schools were completed and the subsequent problems did not help to remove the suspicion with which the estate was already regarded by the city. The unfinished houses and piles of sand and bricks provided attractive play areas for the hundreds of children. Vandalism was rife. The local

16

newspaper wrote:

> For four years acres of unlit building sites, inadequate police supervision, parental apathy and the provision of a public house catering mainly for young people, has provided a perfect setting for the idle, the mischievous, and the more sinister night people.

It was no wonder given the situation of the first tenants many of whom were strangers to the city, and the tone of the public response, that the unsettled families, the teeming children and the lack of amenities made the estate a headache for the welfare services and the police right from the start. And thus from these sources too Omega's unsavoury reputation was confirmed.

By the mid-sixties the association of Omega estate with rough families and criminals was firmly established. A judge sentencing four men from the estate for a property crime was quoted as saying:

> Unless I punish these men, everyone else on the estate will be tempted to have a go won't they?

And even though as always the vast majority of residents were decent hardworking people who resented the reputation of their neighbourhood and suffered from its consequences in daily life, nothing improved over the years. Every incident relating to the estate tended to get exaggerated and used to confirm the existing image. Moreover, as the toddlers grew into teenagers the inadequacies of the estate as a living environment became more sharply focussed.

Every person interviewed in the current research, when asked about the reputation of Omega, said that it was bad. A quarter thought that it shared a bad reputation with two other estates in the city; forty per cent agreed the reputation was bad but felt that it had been manufactured by outsiders, notably the press, and was not deserved. A third of those interviewed told of some way in which this bad reputation affected their lives as residents. The attitudes of workmates often caused distress:

> All the people at work say, oh I wouldn't like to live <u>there</u>. I really hate to have to say where I live.

> I couldn't ask anyone here, I'd feel ashamed.

> I do sometimes feel beyond the pale. I usually tell people that I live near Netherton village.

My workmates call it the reservation.

According to some respondents the address could lose a person a job:

> When I applied I didn't write Omega estate. I wrote
> Netherton. I wouldn't have been given a chance.
> You're all tarred with the same brush here.

> When he gave his address he saw their faces change.
> He didn't get it.

The strategy of giving one's address as the nearby respectable village was commonly used by Omega residents as listings in the telephone directory confirmed:

> It's best not to say Omega estate if you want
> something delivered (from city centre shops) or
> you'll have to wait and be treated badly. Same with
> HP.

The same distrust of the residents was apparently shown by British Telecom:

> I was mad when we moved back to the estate. We'd
> had a phone put in at the other place and we'd never
> been late with our bills, but when we asked to get
> it installed they wanted all the money in advance
> just because of the address. I complained to the
> manager and said it was discrimination and next day
> they came and put it in.

One of the commonest allegations made by residents was that the police treated people differently if they knew they lived on Omega. One complaint was that the police tended to ignore or be very slow in responding to calls coming from the estate. The situations in which residents had asked for intervention by police who had not arrived in time or at all were usually harassment, vandalism, noise, complaints about neighbours, complaints about teenagers. For example the launderette manageress became alarmed one evening when a group of youths refused to leave the premises and used abusive language to her. She telephoned the police station:

> As soon as they took my address I knew they wouldn't
> come. They said they'd be along in five minutes but
> I'm still waiting.

On the other hand there was a widespread belief that the police treated Omega residents with suspicion and dealt with them in a discriminatory fashion. Accusations of this kind came from ultra respectable residents who explained what they regarded as unfair treatment in this way:

18

I've never been in any trouble with the law ever.
But I drove through this broken barrier without
paying the 25p parking charge and they saw me and
when I gave my address they seemed really pleased
and went ahead and did me. I got fined £20.

A grandmother related this example:

My daughter found a bunch of keys and a wallet in
the road. She phoned the police who said to hand
them in. So she sent the lad to the station on his
bike and they kept him for two hours and more or
less accused him of stealing the things and his
mother of covering for him. It hasn't done him a
lot of good I can tell you.

The sensationalising of newsworthy crimes and incidents
however was certainly the most pernicious and pervasive form
of ego-battering for residents of the estate. Of course the
local newspapers reported on pleasant things too, like the
annual fete, a performance by school children or a
charitable collection. But all too often they blew up some
minor incident into an explosion of moral outrage which
shook the whole estate. Newspapers do this anywhere but
there was no doubt that if something happened on Omega
estate it was more likely to get the treatment. There were
some blatant examples of this such as an item headed 'Disco
Night Knifings' concerning the arrest of more than thirty
persons for a brawl in a city centre dance hall, in which
the report referred by name to only three individuals all
with addresses on the Omega estate. Typical of the emotive
scare mongering the estate had to put up with was a story
headed 'Morons' in huge type. The article went on to refer
to 'mindless thugs', 'cowardly attackers', 'moronic muggers'
and 'callous youths'. On the side of the angels was a
'brave pensioner' called 'courageous Sid' who 'dares to walk
the streets of Omega alone at night' and ended up 'battered,
bleeding and broken hearted'. The other side of the story,
which was not printed in the paper, was that Sid was a
disagreeable old troublemaker. He was particularly detested
by teenage youths who liked to use the grassed surround to
the flats for informal games of football, or to gather on
the stairs for a smoke. Sid used to shout at them and
threaten to call the police. One evening they shoved him to
the ground and he scratched his nose on the tarmac. The
implication of the press report that the attack was random
and motiveless and that Omega estate was not safe to walk on
at night was both untruthful and irresponsible.

The most disturbing aspect of the image thus created of

the estate as a dangerous criminal area was that it had been absorbed not just by the rest of the city population but by a considerable number of estate residents who themselves had never personally encountered anything unpleasant but who had read about it in the papers.

One effect of this was fear of going out on the estate at night. In the interviews with residents no question was asked about this so it was a surprise to find that a quarter of respondents spontaneously mentioned at some point that they would never go out alone after dark or allow other family members to do so. One understandable category was the elderly, especially old ladies living alone. They had sometimes been frightened by noise in the street or children banging on the windows or doors. Often however it was:

> I'm afraid of being attacked. It's not like when I was young, I could've walked anywhere on my own. But now you read of all these attacks, it's not safe any more.

The fears were similarly expressed by younger women, often depressed or anxious from years of living with rent arrears, unemployment, and unruly children. A woman who said her nerves were bad and she was 'on tablets' commented:

> It's not safe to go out on this estate at night. It's the sex attacks. I never go out not even to my friend up the street. In fact I very rarely go walking anywhere on the estate at all even in daytime.

The largest category of residents expressing fears about the dangers of the estate at night were those with teenage daughters. Of course parents of adolescent daughters suffer anxieties in whatever social or residential circumstances they live but on Omega there was a sizeable group of parents who perceived the environment of the estate itself as dangerous and threatening and who sought to combat this by exercising a strict and rigid control over their daughters' activities which would be rare indeed in a rural, suburban or middle class milieu. Two sisters for example were never allowed out of doors after dusk unless they were together and had the family Alsatian with them. Then they could walk to the chip shop and back. Numerous parents volunteered the information that they always walked or drove back daughters who had been anywhere on the estate in the evening:

> We always see she gets brought home by her friend's Mum or Dad and we do the same when her friend calls here, she just lives round the corner but we don't

like them to be out after dark on their own, just
the girls, not the boys.

Telephones were seen as very important by these families:

> I must know where they're going and also the
> telephone number so that I can check and make sure
> they've got there.

The parents of an eleven year old girl had just had a
telephone installed:

> so that when she's older she can telephone and we
> can meet her at the bus stop.

The last remark points up the remarkable fact that all these
parents were worried about the dangers of their daughters
walking on the estate at night, not about the dangers of
being on late buses, in the town centre, at licensed discos
or in cars or on motorbikes:

> It's discos all the time, town centre, Burydean,
> Hampton, all over. But we make sure she's taken and
> fetched from the bus. It's too dangerous to walk
> about the estate.

Another girl was allowed anywhere either on the estate or in
town till late if she was on her moped. But if she went
into town on the bus with a friend:

> They must wait at the bus stop under the bright
> light and phone to be picked up in the car.

Since none of the households who expressed these fears of
nighttime attacks had ever personally experienced any
assault or robbery or intimidation one can only assume that
the reputation of the estate built up over the years and the
exaggerations of the press whenever anything did happen were
the cause of the anxieties. One woman who worked an evening
shift said:

> People have the wrong idea about the estate at
> night. I walk back on my own from work every
> evening. I see police patrols sometimes. I'm not
> frightened. I've never been bothered, never seen
> anything at all.

But for most people on Omega the reputation was a factor
to be reckoned with. It caused a vicious circle of events
which acted to make things worse. For it had a direct
effect on the pattern of preferences for different estates
stated by prospective tenants on the housing waiting list,
and also on the list of those wanting transfers and
exchanges. Omega estate was on this count the least popular

of all city estates with both new and existing tenants.
Forty five per cent of residents interviewed had not wanted
to live on the estate but nothing else had been available
when they needed somewhere to live. Over half of these
people said it was the reputation which deterred them. Many
had found it better then they expected and were happy to
stay. Altogether thirty four per cent of those interviewed
did want to leave and go to live elsewhere. It was evident
however that the stigma of the estate must have had an
effect over time on the composition of the population with
increasing numbers living there only because they could not
wait for a preferred estate, or who were desperate to get
out of rented rooms or living with in-laws, or who had been
transferred from somewhere else because they caused trouble
with the neighbours. It was difficult to see how the
reputation could be altered and the process reversed.

3 Omega as a problem estate

The previous chapter has already suggested two factors which had implications for explaining the problem nature of Omega estate. Firstly the longstanding reputation as an undesirable even criminal area resulted in many individuals and indeed whole families suffering humilation in their everyday lives; and often they came to accept the image and feel threatened by the presumed dangers of the estate. Secondly it was inevitable, given the unpopularity of the estate, that a higher proportion of vulnerable families would end up on Omega because they could not wait for a vacancy anywhere else.

It is therefore essential at this point to examine the objective evidence for Omega's description as a problem estate. The usual definition of a 'problem area' is one which has a particularly high incidence of social problems. Thus Amos (1970) in his detailed report on 'social malaise' in Liverpool correlated no less than thirty six malaise indices from crime rates to children deloused, from suicides to the disconnection of electricity supply. Other workers with different objectives have taken only one index, the rate of delinquency, to distinguish between good and bad areas or estates within a city, such as Baldwin and Bottoms (1976) and Herbert (1982). Any housing department identifies its problem estates by the rate of tenant turnover and by the numbers of tenants in rent arrears.

Whatever set of indices is chosen, it is clear that the objective measure of a problem area is in fact the disproportionate amount of work it causes for, and the the high input of resources it demands from, various local authority or government services. Thus while the obvious implication of the term 'problem area' is that the people there have problems, the real meaning of the label is that they cause problems for the authorities.

If for the moment it is agreed that 'causing problems for the authorities' is a justifiable criterion, Omega estate was on all counts a problem area, which was confirmed in the following manner. Statistics were collected, based on the records kept by nearly all the agencies and services involved with residents on the estate in a welfare or controlling role. The only major gap in the statistical coverage concerned demand on the health service. It would of course have been extremely interesting to know whether the incidence of physical and mental illness on Omega estate was worse than in other areas of the city. To explore this fully would have required both interview material and data from records but it was decided not to ask respondents to talk about their health problems as this is a particularly unreliable area about which it was felt that accurate data would be very time consuming to collect. Consequently permission was not asked to consult medical or psychiatric records. For the rest an attempt was made to obtain figures which would allow comparisons between Omega estate and elsewhere in terms of demands on resources. The standard of comparison was another council housing estate called Chalkbury on the same side of the city built at the same time as Omega and which, although only about half the size, had a similar mix of flats and house types. In contrast to Omega Chalkbury had a good reputation. Comparisons were also made between figures for Omega and average figures for the city as a whole. The main comparisons are shown in Table 1.

Social services had an involvement on Omega only approached by one other estate out of the twenty or so administered by the city. The social workers believed it to be their blackest spot and indeed because of this they had a special team concerned only with the estate. Their impression was confirmed by the records. Fifteen per cent of all referrals to them over one year concerned an individual or family on Omega which contained eight per cent of the city households. There were two chief categories of referrals coming from Omega estate: on the one hand referrals related to practical problems of housing, rent

24

Table 1

Problem Profile: Omega, Chalkbury and the City as a Whole (figures for 1981)

Indices	Omega estate	Chalkbury estate	City average	Source
Percentage unemployment among economically active adult males	15	12.5	11	Census 1981
Percentage of single parent households	5.5	3.5	2	Census 1981
Persons per household	3.4	2.8	2.6	Census 1981
Percentage of heads of households classified as in unskilled occupations	44	33	29	Census 1981
Referrals to Social Services in rate per 1000 households	134	115	73	Social Services
Rate per 1000 children 0-16 years in care or under supervision	34	26	17	Social Services
Rate per 1000 juvenile males 10-16 years prosecuted	130	122	85	Social Services
Rate per 1000 adult males prosecuted for criminal offences	70	41	40	Magistrates' Court
Rate per 1000 adult males prosecuted for summary offences	113	93	81	Magistrates' Court
Rate per 1000 households with domestic dispute heard in court	9	4	4	Magistrates' Court
Rate per 1000 adults on orders or licence to probation	12	5	4	Probation Service
Rate per 1000 households on domestic caseload of probation	5	1	1	Probation Service
Cost of repair to five kiosks over six months in pounds sterling	452	242	NK	British Telecom
Rate per 1000 households in serious rent arrears	58	28	33	Housing Department
Rate per 1000 tenancies on waiting list for transfer	47	9	25	Housing Department
Percentage of applicants' stated preferred estates	4	18	NA	Housing Department
Percentage of applicants' stated unwanted estates	35	3	NA	Housing Department
Rate per 1000 households making calls to police station	136	NK	93†	Police records
Rate per 1000 households with reported offences	208	125	160†	Police records

† These averages refer to the police sub-division containing Chalkbury and Omega not to the city as a whole

arrears and threatened evictions, fuel bills, problems with
social security etc. and on the other hand family (including
single parent) problems such as delinquent or truanting
children, quarrels within the family or between neighbours,
accusations of neglect etc. These two categories were
overrepresented on Omega compared with other areas while
referrals related to the elderly or disabled, or the
alcoholic, the homeless etc. were under-represented. The
frequency of problems involving children was clearly
demonstrated by the numbers of Omega children under the
supervision or care of the local authority. Omega estate
accounted for fifteen per cent of city children but provided
thirty per cent of children under local authority
supervision or care. Chalkbury with nearly five per cent of
the juvenile population provided seven per cent of children
looked after by social services.

The high rate of family problems was reflected in the
statistics and case loads of other agencies. The probation
service was responsible for supervision in matrimonial and
custody cases. Omega households were involved at a rate
five times higher than Chalkbury households or households in
other parts of the city. Again eighteen per cent of
magistrates' hearings on domestic disputes involved an Omega
resident while the estate contained only eight per cent of
city households. Calls to the police subdivisional HQ also
reflected the same pattern. Calls reporting domestic
disputes, neighbour disputes or missing or troublesome
children were well over three times as frequent from Omega
than the rest of the subdivision (which included Chalkbury)
and was the largest single category for the estate.

The high proportion of offenders both juvenile and adult
caused work for police, social services, the probation
service and the courts. Seventeen per cent of city
juveniles from ten to sixteen years old lived on the estate
in 1981 but they accounted for twenty five per cent of
juveniles apprehended, and twenty seven per cent of those
prosecuted. With regard to adult offenders passing through
the courts sixteen per cent of adult males prosecuted for
standard list criminal offences came from Omega although
only nine per cent of the adult male population of the city
lived there; whereas Chalkbury with four per cent of the
population housed four per cent of the criminals. However,
looking at summary offences only, which included the large
category of motoring offences and contraventions of
regulations, there were not such dramatic differences. The
offender case load carried by the probation service on Omega
was nearly three times the rate of the city overall; in fact

26

twenty seven per cent of the service's total case load came from the eight per cent of the city households living on Omega estate.

An independent measure of vandalism was obtained from British Telecom who agreed to monitor five telephone kiosks on Omega estate and five kiosks on another council estate. Over a six month period three times as many repair visits had to be made to the Omega boxes and twice as much expense was incurred including the total replacement of three receivers.

Turning now to the housing department, their main concerns were rent collecting, repairs and lettings. Demands for repairs seemed not to differ significantly between estates. In relation to rent arrears, an overall average of three per cent of households were in arrears serious enough and of sufficient longstanding to be brought up before the housing management subcommittee. The rate for Omega was six per cent over two per cent higher than for any other estate. Chalkbury had a rate below three per cent. Omega estate also made work by the numbers of tenants waiting to move out of the estate to alternative council accommodation. Here again it had the highest rate of all estates with five per cent on the official exchange or transfer lists waiting to move elsewhere, while less than one per cent of Chalkbury tenants were waiting to move off their estate. As many as a third of those interviewed said they wanted to move off Omega but most had not taken the necessary official steps as yet. More petitions for the removal of troublesome families came to the department from Omega than from any other estate.

Other indices of resource demand could be seen by looking at the figures for the census taken during the period of the research in April 1981. Unemployment for example meant the payment of unemployment benefit or social security. With fifteen per cent of economically active males unemployed Omega estate had the highest rate for the city in 1981.

Thus it seemed fair to describe the estate of Omega as a problem area if the provisional definition put forward earlier of a problem area as one which demands a disproportionately high level of input of resources by public agencies was accepted. It must not however be taken for granted that this high level of demand for services reflected an exceptionally high need level or high incidence of social problems. The concept of need or of problems is undeniably a relative one whether it is defined by taking objective measures or through the subjective experience of individuals. First it is necessary to consider the possible inadequacies of the objective measures namely the records of those departments and agencies concerned with social care and control.

The lack of evidence for labelling theory (the idea that agencies seek out and record deviancy according to their expectations of an area of bad repute) has already been mentioned in Chapter 1. With regard to police activity for example the researchers found exactly the same as Mawby (1979) that the overwhelming majority of offences became known because victims, witnesses and annoyed residents on the estate telephoned the police, who were in fact often reluctant to come to the scene. The same applied to the high rate of calls for assistance in neighbour and domestic disputes. In the case of social services, departmental records showed that seventy per cent of referrals asking for a social worker came from the individual concerned, someone in the same house, a relative or a neighbour. It was clear that the demand for intervention, the call on resources, was coming for the most part from residents themselves. The high recorded rates of social problems cannot be explained away as a consequence of selective attention by police, social services or other agencies. This led to only two possibilities not necessarily mutually exclusive. One was that the recorded rates faithfully reflected an incidence of social problems which really was higher than for anywhere else (and it seems difficult to explain such things as rent arrears, unemployment figures or the number of single parent households in any other way). Alternatively it could be the case that Omega residents were more ready to report offending persons or disturbing incidents, or more likely to ask for outside help when in difficulties, than people in other estates and areas of the city. Some of the studies discussed in Chapter I indicated that the divisions between tenant lifestyles, particularly where a substantial minority of rough antisocial families were 'imposed' on the respectable conforming majority, were a factor contributing to a high level of intolerance and therefore a high rate of reporting. Research on victimisation (Hood and Sparks, 1970; Sparks et al., 1977) found that reporting of offences was correlated with seriousness of crime, but also with social factors such as confidence in the police. The homogeneity of an area and the social toleration of crime in crime prevalent areas were associated with a low reporting rate. These are nebulous concepts but in the context of Omega estate with a higher than average turnover of tenants, homogeneity and social toleration did seem to be very low.

Thus it is possible that the high level of recorded problems, in some categories at least, was more a consequence of the postwar housing allocation system than a measure of the incidence of real trouble; and that a greater degree of containment and tolerance would be found in areas with lower absolute standards (and lower expectations) but where a greater homogeneity and communality existed. Popplestone and Paris (1979) came to a similar conclusion in their study of difficult council estates in which they considered the distribution of the problems reported to the housing departments:

> What reached the department, therefore, was less a profile of misbehaviour, varying by incidence, than a profile of neighbourhood sensitivity, varying by levels of tolerance, and the degree to which people had faith in the housing department's willingness or ability to change the situation.

One of the Omega residents interviewed made a very similar point:

> It doesn't make any difference where you live, problems are problems. It's just that it gets highlighted more in a place like Omega because somehow it goes outside the family. In other places I've lived, people cope with problems but here the police and social services get involved and it gets spread about. In other places this doesn't seem to happen so much.

To recap therefore, one provisional hypothesis might be that there was a slightly higher proportion of families on Omega compared with other estates who had brought problems with them or who were immature and unstable or who did not want to stay on the estate and so were unsettled; this would have come about through the operation of the normal housing allocation system. In addition, the hypothesis continues, the high rates for the estate of referrals demanding social services intervention, of reported offences, of calls for assistance in domestic and neighbour disputes or for dealing with teenagers' unruliness might be attributable to a low level of tolerance and a readiness to call in authority instead of handling matters at neighbourhood level, rather than to the existence of a very disadvantaged population. If this hypothesis were accepted provisionally it would still be necessary to isolate factors in Omega's situation contributing to this intolerance of others, factors not operative or at least not to such an extent in comparable areas of the city. Homogeneity of the population was one factor suggested by previous work. This and other possible factors will be examined in subsequent chapters which present the views and experiences of Omega residents in relation to life on the estate.

4 Practical problems

Urban living brings with it the need to obtain and maintain
accommodation for oneself and one's family; to get food,
clothes and furniture, and fuel for lighting, heating and
cooking; to have a means of transport from place to place;
and to construct or fit into a social nexus to provide
support in situations such as illness or misfortune when the
individual or family cannot cope alone. The regular
employment of one or more household members normally ensures
that most of the material needs can be met; others must seek
out the various statutory or voluntary agencies operating a
welfare safety net. Even those in work might not be able to
cope with unexpected expenses, or to budget competently on a
limited income. Socially and psychologically some people
are more vulnerable than others, and on these the
environment can sometimes exert intolerable pressures.

Omega estate was defined in the previous chapter as a
problem area measured by the demands from its residents for
intervention by and the input of resources from agencies of
the local administration. Whether or not in objective terms
the practical problems of urban living were really any more
frequent or any worse on Omega than Chalkbury or elsewhere
in the city, people felt they were. And indeed some
indicators of material deprivation were higher on Omega than
other places, for example the unemployment rate, the
proportion of unskilled workers, the large average family

size, the proportion of single parent families and the numbers of households with serious rent arrears. The residents of Omega were not however concerned with statistics but with their experience. Certain practical problems loomed large in conversations and this chapter is concerned with those identified by residents themselves and what they said they did or tried to do to overcome them.

In the early 1980s, over three quarters of the households on the estate were still council tenancies and for these tenants problems with the housing department tended to dwarf all others. Although there was no evidence whatsoever that Omega tenants were treated less efficiently or less urgently than tenants from Chalkbury, Claytown or any of the other score of council estates, for an Omega tenant difficulties with 'the housing' were just one more confirmation that Omega was regarded as a dump. Repairs and maintenance were great flashpoints in tenant-housing department relationships and caused more resentment than any other problem. When repairs were not carried out promptly and properly tenants could not help feeling that it was because people like them did not matter. There may have been all kinds of good reasons why the workmen could not get round to their repair straight away but the tenant, unlike the owner occupier who has been able to discuss the likely timing of the operation with the contractor, was in ignorance of what was going on. Nor was there any sanction like going to another contractor or witholding the rent money for rents and repairs were separately administered by the bureaucracy. Some authorities in England have begun to stipulate time periods within which repairs should be done (e.g. twenty four hours for a request categorised as 'emergency', a week for 'urgent' and between eight weeks and three months for the rest) but only a few have an agreement whereby if these time limits are exceeded the tenant has the right to get the job done privately and send the bill to the council (Housing Research Group 1981). The new Housing and Building Control Act of 1984 was (at the time of writing) expected to give tenants in some circumstances the right to claim back a part of the cost of a private contractor doing repairs but the conditions under which this right could be exercised were restricted and the Act seemed unlikely to substantially help tenants. The repairs problem was compounded on Omega estate by the fact that certain of the dwelling types had structural or design defects which made the occurrence and recurrence of some problems certain. The Omega study showed that of all topics, repairs and maintenance stimulated the most facts and examples as well as a great amount of feeling amongst nearly all respondents.

Nearly eighty per cent of respondents had had to request the housing department to come and do some repair or other, many people several times, since they began the tenancy. Of these almost a half were dissatisfied with the service, often vehemently so; fifteen per cent had no definite views, and the rest felt the service was as good as could be expected. A quarter of the households interviewed stated that there was a repair currently outstanding in the dwelling which they were waiting to be attended to or which was still the same or worse since the workmen had been to see to it. To take one example among many: Ms. Drew was a young divorced mother in employment who lived in one of the downstairs maisonettes, a type of dwelling which was unpopular chiefly for quite obvious design reasons (and which was not common on other city estates). The upstairs maisonette had a balcony which overlooked the scrap of private 'garden' around the front door, the other side of the terraces being open grass with no private enclosed space. The balconies caused trouble because the upstairs people could throw things into the downstairs patch below and because they all had faulty drainage and tended to cause damp or leaking ceilings in the maisonette below. In addition residents complained of the almost total lack of noise insulation between the walls of the maisonettes along a terrace. Ms. Drew had suffered from a leaky ceiling ever since she moved in four years ago and had filled in the rent book card designed for tenants to request repairs on two occasions. Each time:

> a man came to look quite quickly but they have never come back or sent anyone to do anything about it. It doesn't seem worth chasing it up as lots of people have the same problem and they can't do anything.

There were french windows at the other side and these went rotten probably due to being exposed to the weather:

> A couple of years ago they did come to replace them, I thought it was a miracle at the time, but in fact they don't fit at the bottom so I have to lay something along the gap permanently to stop water and draughts. I didn't like to complain seeing as they had taken the trouble to come.

Ms. Drew summed up her feelings about the council repairs department as:

> They are very slapdash, they don't really care.

One of the saddest messages from the things people said about their problems in getting repairs done was that they got the impression that nobody cared about them. They felt lucky if someone came to look at their problem and luckier still if a longstanding repair actually got done. Then if it turned out that the repair was not done properly some people were reluctant to complain. This suggested that the need to battle for repairs to be attended to undermined self respect. Sometimes the system was patently unfair. Ms. Belling had a complaint which was met with on several occasions, that of a broken window which the council apparently would not replace unless she paid for it. The policy seemed to be that whoever broke the window should pay and if a window was broken by, say, a neighbour's child then the tenant should get the money from the neighbour. In Ms. Belling's case the window had been broken in the course of a break-in while the family was away which had been reported to the police. It was a large window and would cost a lot of money so there was deadlock between Ms. Belling and the council over the problem, while of course it was Ms. Belling and her family who were suffering from the inconvenience.

The supposed reciprocity of obligations between council and tenant was mentioned by a number of people who expressed clearly their resentment that they were expected to pay the rent promptly or expect immediate consequences while the housing department could allow long delays to build up or do shoddy work with no possibility of retribution. As Mrs. Jordan said:

> They're quick enough to send you a letter if you're a week late with the rent but they never do the repairs or if they do them, they're not done properly. They put the rents sky high and still don't do the repairs.

Some of the older tenants in fact did not always realise the extent to which the council landlord was responsible. For example Mrs. Berry was an elderly widow living in a small ground floor flat in a block which had a number of retired persons but also a few young couples. She was not hostile to the council and indeed made the point that whenever the lights in the entrance passage to the flats got broken which was very frequently and which were of great importance to the elderly folk going in and out and up the stairs, that the workmen invariably came to fix them the very next day. But this old lady had to put up day by day with window catches which did not work, a kitchen window which was rotten at the corner and which she dared not open for fear it fell to bits, and outside plastic drainpipes which had been broken off by children and made everywhere wet. All these had, she said, been reported by telephone but she had not had any visits from workmen though she was in all day. She also had cracks in the kitchen wall which the workmen eventually arrived to repair. They then 'made good' by repainting the wall but did so in a different colour which did not match the rest of the kitchen. The old lady herself did not really blame the council but seemed to feel the failure was more that of her son who lived nearby but for whom she made excuses:

Well, he has his own family doesn't he?

Whatever the reasons for the council's apparent lack of efficiency with regard to repairs, there was clearly a desperate lack of a communications channel between the repairs and works departments and the estate residents, and this silent delay was perceived by tenants as not caring and treating their needs and complaints as unimportant. This perception was reinforced by certain other experiences they had or had heard about. For example when someone made the effort to approach one of the local councillors, either privately or at the weekly 'surgery' in the community centre, things usually got moving and people heard about this. Mrs. Disley said:

He was very helpful. Mam's windows were broken for about three months and he got them fixed the day after we went to see him.

Mr. Dale's house had a leaking roof for three years during which council workmen had visited twice but not improved the situation. Mr. Dale contacted one of the councillors whom he knew from his work and who was in the same union and the workmen came again very soon. He was also able to obtain a new parkray and boiler free of charge on the grounds that the previous tenants had been responsible for the damage to the first one. This was entirely just of course but his experience contrasted with that of others who were not believed when they complained of cracks they had not caused. An active elderly widow, Mrs. Knight, who became friendly with the woman councillor by attending pensioners' coffee mornings said when she had a repair problem (her most recent one had been blocked gutters) she telephoned the councillor and found that things were put right within a day, whereas waiting for gutters to be unblocked was mentioned as taking a period of years by other respondents. When people saw that councillors' intervention got things done immediately which would not be done for months or years by normal processes, the inference drawn was not so much that the councillor had got them what they were anyway entitled to, but rather that the council could be manipulated by personal influence, you had to be Mr. Bigshot with the power to make things difficult for the officials in the housing department. Several respondents expressed the belief that the council did not care, did not want to know, and ignored their requests and many others obviously felt this to judge from their answers.

The gap in communications between department and tenant was referred to above. In fact there was considerable evidence that personal contact was an important variable in getting things done and that lack of personal contact was seen by tenants as a reason for repairs not getting done or being delayed. Those who realised this were able to get better results. Mr. Merton said he had no trouble getting repairs done. He then went on to explain his methods:

> If you send the card in you'd wait months or for ever. It's best to call in and see someone at the central city offices and then ring up in a few days and then keep ringing back and ask for the person you saw. They'll send someone. As with anything else, those that shout loudest get most.

Several people made the same point as Mrs. Lake who said:

> Until a few years ago the rent man called and you could tell him when things needed doing. He would take notice of the condition of the house and garden. Now no-one checks up, so some people don't bother any more.

In principle the channel of communication with the tear-off repairs request card attached to the rent book could potentially have been as or more efficient than when the rent man called. But the difference probably lay in the feeling of personal responsiblity the rent man himself would have had, knowing that he would soon be face to face with the family once again; and from the tenants' point of view it could well be that merely the assurances of the rent man that things were under way would forestall the build-up of frustration caused by several weeks or months with no communication.

'Shouting loudest' and an attempt to personalise the contact was one response which tenants made to the repairs situation. Another was to Do-It-Yourself. About a third of respondents in fact did at least some of the necessary repairs themselves at their own cost. Some were driven to doing so after lengthy dissatisfaction with what the council did. The Snape family had had two bad experiences both of which they solved finally only by doing things themselves at their own cost. They had spent one miserable winter (they had two young children) with a parkray with a back boiler which was broken. According to Mrs. Snape the process lasted a year, with the council saying they would come to mend the boiler on such and such a day and for them not to light the fire. The workmen would then not come on that day but turn up unannounced on a later day when the fire was lit again and they could not do any work on it. When the next winter was approaching and the fire still was not in working order Mr. and Mrs. Snape went out and bought a gas fire themselves. They asked the council if they would pay half the cost but they refused. The other main hassle they had had concerned a number of badly cracked tiles on the kitchen floor. They managed to get someone to come and replace the damaged tiles but they put in a different type which did not match and ruined the look of the kitchen. Again Mr. and Mrs. Snape asked if the council would pay something towards the cost of a new floor covering but in the end the family recovered the floor with vinyl tiles at their own expense.

Others seemed to take a positive pride in not being dependent on the council for repairs. For example, Mr. Last, who worked as a builder's labourer, said he was quite happy with the housing department and had no grumbles. Earlier in the interview he had already commented that he liked to be selfsufficient, he kept himself to himself and never went to others for help. Later it transpired that over the two years he and his wife had been in their house, Mr. Last had seen to a leaking cistern and reboxed this cistern and had renewed a rotting back door.

Some respondents showed that they were aware of the difficulties of manpower and resources which the council could be facing but thought that in that case greater flexibility in the rules would be reasonable. As Mrs. Jordan said:

> What's ridiculous is that they won't let you do what you'd like to do yourself.

This was a reference to the ruling that any improvements or alterations or replacements with other than standard fittings in theory had to be put back as they were before if the tenant left. In practice nothing unreasonable would have been taken as far as that by the council, certainly not a new door or sink unit put in at the expense of the tenant, but the regulations were there and acted as a deterrent to initiative. The rules applied also to external painting, the responsibility of the council, but Mr. Dale, a great decorator in his spare time, had painted his front door a different colour from everyone else's and had had no repercussions. Another family, Mr. and Mrs. Morgan, suggested that where tenants were willing the works department could supply the parts, the new door, the new glass for a window, the gate hinges or even the paint and people could do the jobs themselves. This did seem an eminently sensible compromise between tenants being driven to footing large bills themselves and frustrating periods of inconvenience and delay. In some cases though, even when a tenant was keen and willing to make an improvement at his own expense (and surely in the council's ultimate interest), obstacles seemed to be needlessly put in the way. Mr. Overton wanted to build a small extension and patio on the back of his house similar to one already built onto the house next door. He had been trying to get permission for six months:

> They've given me so much red tape it's putting me off, took months to get a reply to my first letter and I wouldn't have got that except I called in and phoned several times. I described exactly what I wanted to do, build one wall, but they seemed to think I wanted to knock walls down, they did'nt come to look. Now the summer's gone and you can't do something like that in the winter. I don't know whether to forget about it altogether or keep on and on and maybe get the go-ahead for next summer.

The saddest response to the frustration of waiting for years for repairs to be done was the one mentioned above by Mr. and Mrs. Lane:

> Some people don't bother any more.

Some residents did just give up. Mr. and Mrs. Rowlands lived on a corner adjacent to waste land and the original fencing round the back garden had been falling to bits for the last ten years:

> It's like a public thoroughfare. We can't do anything with the garden because we can't keep them out. We've complained time and time again, phone calls and visits to the office on several occasions but they've done nothing about it. We're fed up with shouting at kids to keep out but they regard it as public because there's no fence. We pay £20 a week now but they do nothing. I've lost heart, it's a tip now, it needs a strong fence. We're not doing anything till they put up a fence.

One common cause of the dissatisfaction of many residents was the quality of the external painting done every seven years or so. Respondents said that the workmen simply painted over the old paint even when it was cracked and blistered or when the wooden structures were rotting or damaged with the not unexpected consequence that the new paint frequently just peeled off again. Mrs. Cope said:

> There's no supervision of the men, no check on the work.

Most people agreed that for electrical faults the council's response was very quick. But it seemed that even then the aim was to cure the immediate symptom rather than get to the root of the problem. A frequent occurrence, Mr. Cope said, was an electric light bulb 'blowing out', a minor explosion which damaged and blackened the socket. The council repairmen came quickly to replace the socket and bulb but did nothing to examine the cause of the recurring phenomenon.

Another context in which tenants had to interact with the housing department in order to get something done was when they wanted an allocation or transfer. Twelve per cent of respondent families were either on the transfer list or else were advertising for an exchange hoping to be able to move off the estate. In fact a third of the sample said they would like to move away but less than half of these had taken any steps towards doing so for various reasons. Some people told of experiences with getting allocated or transferred to their present dwelling. Exactly the same frustrations and problems had arisen as with repairs. There had been long waits without any communication and the coming up against regulations which seemed meaningless from the tenant's point of view. And the same remedies were used, for example making a constant nuisance of oneself and procuring the intervention of an influential third party. Housing transfers were the single largest category of problem for which respondents approached a councillor. In some cases this amounted to the councillor doing virtually all the work him or herself. The councillor of course, knowing the ropes, was able to bridge the communications gap by explaining to the tenant the procedure to be followed, and was often able to co-ordinate the various stages on a personal basis. For example the Samson family had lived on one of the busy main roads on the estate. They wanted to move and if possible to leave Omega altogether. They enlisted the help of a councillor:

He was very good. He got all the health visitor,
social worker, and doctor's reports together and
gave them to housing. It took all of them to get
the move into here, and they were still reluctant
and told us we had to take this one (which is still
on the estate) or we'd wait at least three years to
get off.

One rule greatly resented by some tenants was that which
said that no transfer was possible while rent arrears were
owed although some cases were known in fact to occur. This
rule was difficult to understand since as Mr. Donaldson put
it:

The National Assistance pay our rent plus arrears
for us anyway so no matter where we move it'll be
paid so why won't they let us move?

There seemed no clear reason why someone should not be
allowed to move to lower rent or even same rent
accommodation but many tenants had been caught in this trap.
Ms. Pearson wanted to move back to Omega, where her family
lived, with her two babies after the break-up of her
relationship with her boyfriend. The boyfriend had not paid
the rent and a court case came up followed by the bailiff to
evict the family since by then the man had disappeared with
no payments made. In the end Ms. Pearson was allowed to
remain on condition she paid off the arrears bit by bit. It
was not made plain to her at first that she could not hope
to move with arrears outstanding:

They told a lot of lies, you'll be moved in a few
months and nothing happens, then when you keep
asking, then they mention the arrears. All you want
to know is the truth. You would rather know you'd
got to wait two or three years than keep living in
false hopes.

This same young woman got another nasty shock, when she
thought she had paid off the arrears, to receive a
computerised statement to the effect that she still owed
over £50. She then went to one of the councillors who,
while he could not help to change the circumstances, was
able to explain that she was liable for the court costs in
addition to the arrears since her cohabitee could not be
found. The councillor explained the situation and exactly
what she had to do to be eligible for her much wanted
transfer, which she then successfully accomplished.

An example of individual initiative was the case of
Mrs. Arthur. She and her husband had been five years on the

waiting list for a first tenancy presumably because having only one child they had not accumulated extra points. Finally they were told they were getting close to the top of the list but still no offers were made for months. So one day Mrs. Arthur set off:

> I went all round Omega and wrote down the addresses of all the empty houses and maisonettes. Then I went straight and told the man in the council office that I was not leaving that office till we got a place to live. I got the keys of this place in 30 minutes. Mind you, it was in an awful state. It's taken us six months to get it clean and decorated.

This young couple were desperate since living with their in-laws was becoming increasingly impossible. Although they would have preferred some other estate Mrs. Arthur was being realistic in using as her ammunition the void dwellings on Omega estate.

These illustrations of tenant-housing department relations were of course taken chiefly from the forty five per cent of respondents who held a low opinion of the housing department. Others were resigned to putting up with delays and inefficiencies and yet others with particular initiative (or a bit more money) managed to avoid being dependent on council bureaucracy for every bit of maintenance or every transaction.

At the end of Chapter 2 the point was made that Omega badly needed a new image, an improved reputation, for so many other problems were a consequence of its reputation. Work on the Priority Estates Project by the Department of the Environment (Hedges et al. 1980, Power 1981, 1982, 1984) cited in Chapter 1 found that expediting repairs to the insides of houses and giving tenants a say in what other improvements were attempted on the estates increased the self respect of residents and that in turn appeared to lead to them taking greater responsibility in other things. From their experiments the answer seemed to lie in de-centralising the housing department into estate or neighbourhood offices as Walsall did in 1982 (Seabrook 1984) where individual housing officers could take responsibility for all the different services for tenants, whether a request for repairs, a transfer application, a tenancy for a relative or how to cope with rent arrears. This method got over the communications gap and the feeling of impersonality. Repairs could still take a long time (though that too could be speeded up if repairs teams became estate based as in Walsall) and it could still be years to get a vacancy but if the tenant could call into the local office and talk to the officer who knew about the case and who was acquainted with any developments, then he or she could feel informed, in control, and a citizen with rights; he or she would be less likely to feel resentful, hostile and alienated.

Another familiar problem related to living on Omega was that of rent arrears. The rate was much higher than for any other estate yet the rents were the same as anywhere else for comparable accommodation. Nor were rent arrears a new problem introduced by increased unemployment. Rent arrears were a problem characteristic of the estate even in the early days when it housed a high percentage of well paid skilled workers. One explanation for the continuing problem was that it could have been a side effect of the type of accommodation built, in that the estate always housed a predominance of very large families. In the sixties the average household size was 4.3 compared with 3.2 for the city as a whole and in the 1981 census it was 3.4 compared with 2.6.

Eight respondent families admitted they were in arrears and were prepared to talk about it. None of them could have been regarded as 'problem' families in the sense that they caused trouble in the neighbourhood, or in the sense of having multiple problems requiring intervention. In all these households there had been an economic precipitating factor such as marital separation or the husband losing his job. Only Mr. Donaldson (who possibly supplemented his income unofficially) was running a car. None of them seemed to go out for recreation at all. As Mr. Sawyer who had four children said:

> We can't afford to go out. We spend £18 on rent (of which £2.40 was arrears), £13 on the electricity meter, £10 on buses to town, a bit on the gas, and that doesn't leave enough to live on when you've bought food and you can't have the children going without.

Or Mrs. Kent:

> We can't afford to go anywhere. We used to enjoy going into town and looking round the shops but now it's 84p on the bus and I've better things to do with the money.

Mr. Donaldson said:

> I haven't been in a pub in two years, and that's

something for a Scot to admit.

Ms. Redder's three children of nine, ten and fifteen badly needed new shoes, coats and sports gear. But children were the last to be deprived. Ms. Pearson managed to scrape and save enough to buy a secondhand pushchair so that she could take the baby out with her little boy, and Mr. and Mrs. Donaldson had managed to afford to let the two middle children go on a school trip. Keeping an allotment, home decorating, knitting, sewing, were various ways members of these families used their time constructively.

It appeared, therefore, that the families on Omega who were in financial difficulties were taking the matter seriously and trying very hard to keep within their limited means. There may well of course have been families on the estate who did not act responsibly. Residents sometimes referred to these people who were reputed to get unlimited help when they did not deserve it. But they were not typical of the ordinary Omega resident in difficulties with the budget.

It was of interest to consider the attitudes of these families to the experience of being in rent arrears. None of the families in arrears seemed to feel ashamed of the fact, probably because they could point to a good reason why it had come about e.g. unemployment or separation from the breadwinner, so they did not feel it was their own personal failings; also they knew of other families in the same position. The Sawyer family, for example, had in their possession a copy of a court order made on a neighbour requiring him to pay only 95p per week on a debt of £300 while Mr. Sawyer was supposed to pay £2.40p on similar arrears. Mr. Sawyer was keeping this as evidence in case they did not manage to keep up the extra amount and were taken back to court. Once the mechanics of repayment had been sorted out, either by the DHSS taking over payments direct, or the residents making their own arrangements, being in rent arrears did not appear to be a source of distress to the respondent families. But there was some bitterness expressed by some of the families that the welfare agencies had not been able to provide more help in the form of household goods or vouchers for food or clothing. That these kinds of material aid did exist they knew well. They also seemed aware that the social services were being cut back, nevertheless the feeling remained as Mrs. Donaldson put it that:

Other people seem to get everything.

It seemed however, that none of the families had been

43

totally without the aid of some representative of the welfare services.

In general it could be said that the insolvent families were still aware of their rights in all respects and did not feel that being in arrears with rent or bills altered their rights in any way. In fact it increased them to the extent that they were more, not less, deserving of whatever extra benefits were allegedly available. At the same time all were doing there best to cope on their limited means.

While the problem of rent arrears was only discussed by eight families, a higher proportion was faced with the wider problem of unemployment. Fourteen per cent of male heads of households of working age in the Omega sample were registered unemployed and seeking work, and no less than sixty per cent of female heads of households had no paid employment; there was also a small group of respondents who, though of working age, were chronically sick. The unemployment rate for economically active males on the estate was fifteen per cent according to the 1981 census.

The clear impression from talking to these families was that there was no stigma attached to being unemployed. Respondents seemed to be quite frank in admitting they had been laid off or made redundant or could not find a job. Attitudes may well have changed towards being unemployed over the recent years of increasing unemployment at all class and SEG levels owing to the constant comment and analysis in the media. Some evidence that this had happened was provided by Mrs. Overton's account of her husband's experience some years back:

> He was ill when we first moved here in the early seventies and he had been written off at work. Next door called him a scrounger and he's never got over that. He had an accident and every now and again his back goes. He's a really hard worker and he was very upset so he never bothered with anyone after that.

Some of the unemployed men had, it seemed, accepted voluntary redundancy which probably meant they had received a lump sum payment. These and other families where either the wife or grown up children were in fulltime employment were still running cars. They were managing and did not appear to have had to restrict their activities. The other families with unemployed male heads were somewhat hard pressed and all had contact with some agency worker such as a health visitor, local authority social worker or the welfare officer from the factory where they had been employed. There was no indication that they were getting any material help from these sources other than advice on entitlements such as rent rebate. Though one cannot generalise from the relatively few families in this category (working age, male head unemployed, no capital or other income, dependent children) it was encouraging that none were without any monitoring contact or unaware of their general right to benefits.

On the other hand, the whole question of rights and benefits gave rise to conflicting feelings and sometimes bitterness. The overall impression gained from talking to the families of the unemployed men was that while, as was stated before, they did not appear to feel shame or stigma, there was nevertheless a pride, a value put on being able to manage without welfare help; yet at the same time, a sense that some people less deserving and provident than themselves got a lot of benefits coming their way as a result of their improvidence. As Mrs. Sands said:

> It's not right that Pat (her anti-social neighbour) gets her rent paid while people like us ask for nothing, even though my husband's been made redundant, we manage on our own.

Mr. Brewster was perhaps the most sensitive of the respondents about his unemployment. He was scathing towards the man next door who 'won't bloody work' and bitter about his own situation:

> It's this Government, soon there'll be nothing, a man out of work, how will he start again after two or three years on the dole? It's worse for those trying to be good and respectable. When unemployment is bad, people get money trouble and go out and steal. You want it to be seen that you can provide for your family.

Mr. and Mrs. Webster were proud that they had never had anything to do with any form of helping agency believing everyone had to rely on themselves. Mr. Webster put this into practice by filling his time decorating and maintaining the house, and doing the housework and cooking while his wife and son and daughter-in-law went out to work.

There were a few households where the man was permanently unemployed through longterm illness. For these there was little prospect of things improving. Mr. and Mrs. Freeman were approaching retiring age. He had been able to work very little over the past twenty years and they had adapted to a simple lifestyle of staying at home and sometimes having in friends from their Jehovah's Witness church who obviously were a moral support to them. The health visitor was also regularly in touch and provided medical aids for the sick husband. This couple had few expectations and while they commented on how dear the rent was they were quite contented in their way. In contrast were two men in their late fifties, Mr. Aston and Mr. Brown, both divorced, alone, unable to work, and living surrounded by people who all belonged to families. Totally isolated and friendless, these men had nothing to do but go out drinking or sit at home and watch television. Both hated the estate and it seemed everyone ignored them. Mr. Brown said:

> When I can afford it, I just go up to the pub, I buy
> a few 'Hellos' by buying a drink. I have to buy
> companionship.

Neither were in contact with any agency and did not seek such contact, in fact would no doubt have been hostile to attempts to visit or befriend them. However both wanted to move from the estate into more city-like surroundings but both seemed to have found getting anything done in this direction was complicated and involved long waits with no idea if anything was happening.

Another relatively disadvantaged group was the ten per cent of households consisting of single mothers, a growing category which suffered particular problems of its own. A few of the single mothers were divorced women in their thirties or forties with school or teenage children. Three of these mothers had jobs but only one managed to run a car and she was unusual in having a son also in fulltime employment. The majority were young women in their early twenties who had not been married at all or who had married and divorced almost before they were out of their teens. Only one of this group had a car and a job. Typically the features which the majority of these single mothers shared were: no paid employment if the child or children were pre-school, one reason being the lack of day nursery places and the fact that the local playgroup in the community centre took children either mornings or afternoons only; no car; very little or no social life outside the house; and the likelihood of being in regular contact with a health visitor or social worker. Isolation from neighbours was also noted but on the other hand most of the single mothers had their own relatives living not far away and in regular contact. While surprisingly none of these mentioned practical help in the way of babyminding by these relatives, visiting and being visited did seem to be the mainstay of the mothers' social lives. All those with only one child had been allocated a flat or maisonette rather than a house, and this must have seemed a reasonable policy from the council's point of view. But Ms. Drew felt this was wrong:

> Single parent families are on the increase but they always put them in flats. This is wrong, they need a house and garden as much or more than a proper family. Why should they discriminate against the kids? It's not their fault.

The single parents in the sample certainly could not turn to their neighbours for help with the day to day practicalities of life. This might have been because of neighbours' disapproval or else because there was no built-in basis of reciprocity and neighbours feared they would be put upon if they offered help. It was remarkable that only one of the single mothers said that she had helpful and friendly neighbours. She had only recently been divorced, had lived on the estate for seventeen years and brought up four children in the house she was still living in. All the others said they had very little to do with their neighbours or that they were definitely unfriendly. Ms. Field in a block of twelve flats, four facing onto each floor, said:

> Don't know any of them at all.

Ms. Drew lived in a row of compact maisonettes:

> They all keep themselves to themselves and that suits me.

Ms. Bingham heard that one who had been a friend had talked about her saying her children were out of control.

> That really hurt me so I don't bother with them anymore, I just say 'hello'. They think if you're on your own you're an easy target, they run you down because there's no man to stick up for you.

Ms. Belling:

> We say 'hello' both sides but I don't know anyone else. The woman next door was at school with me but she hasn't acknowledged this, so though I know her first name I wouldn't use it.

Ms. Worrell:

> I don't mingle much. I haven't found the neighbours at all friendly. I say 'Good Morning' to next door on the right and that's it.

What help these women did receive invariably came from friends and acquaintances living elsewhere on the estate who were in the same situation. Ms. Worthy:

> Carole, a couple of streets away, I work with her, she calls here and vice versa. I borrow her car to do my shopping.

Ms. Pearson:

> Well, there's Sue, she's on her own as well and she has kids of the same age. She calls every day or else I call in to see her just in passing on my way to the shops. She was here last night and looked after the kids.

Ms. Redder:

> This bit is very snobbish so I don't bother with the neighbours, but I have about twenty friends on the estate, most of them like me, on their own with kids. I think people like us stick together. None of them are neighbours but I go to Christine's all the time. It's the only place I do go since he left.

Ms. Drew:

> The only one I have anything to do with is Jean, she comes in every day and takes him to playschool and looks after him until I get back from work. I mind her little girl when she goes out.

Even Ms. Field who said she knew no neighbours at all had a friend she described as 'another Mum' on the other side of the estate who came to mind her child once or twice a week. In the sample was one male single parent with a nine year old daughter to look after. He had a considerable problem because he was employed at the factory and expected to do shifts. Mr. Pratt said about his neighbours (and he had lived in the house for eleven years):

> They knew I had a problem but nobody offered and I didn't think they would be helpful so I didn't ask.

Instead he had approached the factory welfare officer and asked if they could find someone to look after his daughter before and after school. He said:

> They couldn't help, they have people with lots of problems now and my daughter was older and only one and some of the workers have big families of small children to cope with. So I had to ask permission to come in late in the mornings, which I did, and then they docked the money from my pay.

Mr. Pratt admitted that he had not really tried the

neighbours:

> It's not in my character to ask, but nobody offered.
> It's not easy to make friends here.

And yet this man had said earlier that while he only knew two families in the whole road there was a divorced woman over the way who would come over to ask him to help when she needed household jobs doing like fixing and mending things. If he had asked he might have received help.

Considering the single parent families as a group it was clear that the greatest problem they faced was getting someone to look after their child or children whether they went out to work or just wanted to go into town or out for the evening or if they were ill. It must surely be the deepseated feeling that a helping relationship must be potentially reciprocal that determined the marked coolness of relations between single parents and their neighbours. The neighbours feared getting involved lest they should find themselves imposed upon, and the single parents were unwilling to ask for help lest they should be thought unable to manage.

As has already been indicated there was evidence that persons or families with serious problems of a material nature such as longterm rent arrears, or the worst off among the unemployed or chronic sick, or the single mothers with young children, had been in contact at some point with a social worker or a health visitor. They had received advice, help with bureaucratic procedures and occasionally material help. The social services were involved in any one year with about one in ten of Omega households, and the health visitors were automatically responsible for at least occasional visits to all families with preschool children and the chronic sick and elderly infirm. There may have been families or persons in other kinds of distress who never came to the notice of welfare agencies such as the isolated Mr. Brown referred to earlier, but in his case he would have refused interference and it would have been difficult to solve his problems.

Although Omega could not be said to have a community spirit except within small localised patches, there was evidence of a kind of remote vigilance which often led to referrals being made to the welfare agencies without any personal contact between the referrer and referred. When Mrs. Higgins, for example, heard a child screaming continously late one night she watched out of the window until she saw the mother return from the pub:

49

I rang the health visitor the next day and I think
she must have done something because it hasn't
happened again.

Mrs. Trapp was slightly anxious abut an elderly couple
living nearby:

Nowadays you never know what to do, whether to offer
help or stay away because you'd be intruding.
Elderly people over the years have got very proud
and they don't want help so they stay lonely. I
don't know how much help social services can give
but I'd give them a ring if I got worried.

The implication was that help from social services might be
more acceptable because more anonymous than 'intrusion' by a
neighbour.

Attitudes to social services among residents were
distinctly different between those who were or had been
clients and those who had not. It seemed as if here was
another dividing line between those who perceived themselves
as the hardworking respectable working class and the rest.
For the respectables there was a stigma attached to the
'welfare'. Mrs. Wyatt in a voice which defied further
discussion said:

No, I don't know anything about them and I don't
wish to.

Mrs. Noakes said firmly:

If I ever need any help I'd go to my doctor not to
any social worker.

Others expressed negative views typical of many.
Mr. Higgins said:

People go along and say they've got problems and
they get more help than people who try and cope by
themselves.

Mrs. Gatehouse said:

The welfare comes every week to see the woman and
kids next door but it doesn't do her any good.

Others seemed almost to be blaming social workers for the
continuing problems of the estate. Mr. Lane said:

We've a number of neighbours with domestic problems,
they all have visits by social workers, but they've
still got their problems. There's a father over
there, left with the children to look after, they

promised they'd help but nothing has happened.

And Mrs. Mulpepper:

> All they do is make excuses for young thugs, say
> it's because they're deprived or had an unhappy
> childhood. They learn that whatever they do they
> don't get punished so there's no deterrent, is
> there?

On the other hand the attitude of those with first-hand
experience of social services contact was quite plainly that
the social services were there to provide material and
practical aid to deserving folk having difficulty making
ends meet. Their views also tended towards the negative but
in terms of not giving out enough or giving it to the wrong
people. Ms. Redder was an experienced client who had
realised the constraints within which social services were
currently operating:

> They used to be alright years ago when I first had
> one, they cared about and helped me and my kids, but
> now they just say they can't help, cutbacks, etc.
> They're alright in that they'll listen and they'll
> give advice about electricity and rent arrears, she
> got in touch with social security for me, and they
> took over, but you can't get any financial help from
> them at all. Now anything you get you have to pay
> back. They used to give you food parcels years ago
> and second-hand furniture. I wanted a grant for
> clothes but the welfare woman says they don't do
> this sort of thing any more.

Others made no allowances. Mrs. Donaldson said:

> When she calls she can't get out quick enough. She
> calls to see Gordon, he wets the bed and she's
> trying to help. She gave us a buzzer but when we
> needed a new mattress she took the buzzer away and
> hasn't been back. Other people seem to get
> everything. We never get any real help. I asked
> about a pram and all she said was to try the 'Under
> a Tenner' in the paper.

Ms. Field had had a lifelong involvement with social
workers:

> I dunno what they're supposed to do. Never told me
> anything I didn't know. Only thing I ever wanted
> was to get her a place in a nursery. She came round
> to see me but didn't do a thing. A waste of time.
> Never had any help.

Health visitors too came in for the same kinds of criticism.

Mrs. Roper with four children had wanted to move to a bigger house:

> They should help you but they don't. He (the youngest boy) gets very bad asthma and he needs a room of his own. I went to the health visitor and wanted her to help us get moved. She just said she couldn't help.

Mrs. Riley similarly felt resentful when she wanted a place for her four year old in a nursery. She was told nothing could be done for a year:

> It's discrimination. I know she has helped other families who've only got two children.

Other clients and particularly the sick or elderly felt a positive benefit from the health visitor's contacts and although they always listed the practical aid they received it was clear the health visitor's role was more widely supportive than they perhaps realised. Thus Mrs. Rogers had been given a bath rail and a telephone and the health visitor organised the payment of her rent by giro. For Mrs. Enworthy who was disabled, the health visitor had arranged occupational therapy classes, a bath frame, a rail in the entrance of the flats, a Christmas shopping trip and obtained information about art classes. All the elderly or disabled respondents had had some contact. Mrs. Freeman said:

> They're nice. They come to see my husband. They've got lots of aids to help him get up out of bed or in the bath. Any other little things they think he could use they bring for him. Very good to him they are, and they always call in on us if they're round here.

The role of the health visitor was less easily misconstrued and even non-clients with no first hand experience were less willing to express condemnatory opinions. This may have been because it was generally appreciated that everybody in certain categories was visited, thus there was no stigma as there was with being referred to a social worker; or it may have been that the idea of responsibility for the health of babies or the comfort of the sick and elderly was a simpler one to grasp. Feelings by and large were favourable and there were no derogatory comments made about pandering to scroungers. However the image of welfare workers first and foremost among clients and non-clients alike was of the gatekeepers to practical and material aid, deserved or undeserved according to viewpoint.

Although on Omega it seemed probable that between them the agencies were reaching the majority of those most entitled to or who sought such help, the stigma of social services in the minds of the self reliant and the respectable acted in a divisive way. The role of social services was unclear and confused in many respondents' minds and the fact that the service operated from a central city office made matters worse. What Omega really needed was an open friendly office on the estate to give welfare rights advice and which could take referrals and deal with the practical problems of clients such as sorting out arrears payments. In some areas of the country such social work teams have been attached to local health centres and this has worked out well. Understanding of the help they give, access and convenience for residents, liaison between the agencies, and above all the image, could be improved this way. What is being suggested above of course is not new, it is the decentralisation of social services into neighbourhood 'patches'. The argument has been forcefully put in their review of social welfare policies by Hadley and Hatch (1981):

> The application of a strategy . . . . must be designed to
> (1) enable front line staff to have detailed knowledge of the area served, including its informal caring networks, relevant local and statutory organisations and their opposite numbers in the staff of these organisations;
> (2) facilitate easy access by users to the team at the local level;
> (3) ensure that the team has the authority and capacity to respond rapidly at local level in providing help.
> These requirements lead logically to the decentralisation of services to small areas of perhaps 5,000-10,000 and, ideally, the establishment on such 'patches' of small integrated teams of social workers, ancillaries, home helps, wardens and volunteers.

Earlier in this chapter the same local devolution was suggested for council housing management to combat the remoteness and helplessness of residents faced with problems of repairs, arrears and transfers etc. Indeed a neighbourhood housing office could be an equally suitable place for welfare rights advisers and for social workers to operate from. A familiar and welcoming drop in centre to cater for all the various practical problems which arose in the lives of Omega residents could be a step towards a shared feeling of community and perhaps community responsibility.

5 Neighbour trouble

Neighbour disputes were a particular feature of life on Omega estate. As was reported in Chapter 3 calls to the police for this reason showed a rate three times that for the rest of the city subdivision. Petitions to the housing department also reflected the extent of the problem. When Omega residents were interviewed forty per cent said that they had a current situation with troublesome neighbours and a further thirteen per cent had experienced the same over recent years but the families concerned had moved or been moved. In each small locality of the estate the same households were identified again and again as being a source of trouble. Among all the factors analysed from the interview data the one most highly and significantly correlated with dissatisfaction with one's neighbourhood was having one or more 'troublesome neighbours'. The problem was therefore a considerable one which could affect the atmosphere and wellbeing of a whole road or block and the immediate vicinity. Eighty per cent of those with no neighbour problem were content with life on Omega while more than half of those who identified a nearby household as a problem to others were unhappy and many of them said they wanted to move off the estate altogether. Of all the problems described by estate residents this one caused more distress, fear and misery on a day to day basis than any other and, unlike with the practical problems discussed in the last chapter, there were no routine procedures to go through to improve the situation.

The problem in the form of a public responsibility has been with us as long as there have been council estates. Council policies designed to deal with or prevent the problem have varied over time and between authorities, but the social engineering was still not right while something like half the households on an estate like Omega currently or recently had suffered from nuisance or harassment from other people.

What kind of people caused these problems? And what exactly did they do? 'A problem family lives above me' said Mr. Little whose experience of neighbour trouble will be described later. But the question which must be addressed is whether the frequency of the troublesome neighbour syndrome on Omega estate was really caused by the slightly higher proportion of the more vulnerable and disadvantaged families living there, and indeed whether such people deserved the label of problem families anyway. The term was so often used when discussing the estate by both outsiders and residents that it was evident that it was necessary to define it carefully.

In Chapter 3 the question arose of the definition of 'problem estate' and it was decided that the term really meant an area that caused problems for the authorities in the amount of work and resources it demanded. The same principle could be applied in relation to the use of the term 'problem family' so that a problem family would be one with a high level of involvement by the various agencies and services such as police, social services, probation, DHSS and the housing department. Amos (1970) found a very high correlation between many different indices of what he called 'social malaise' which would require intervention by the authorities mentioned above such as children in care, truancy, crimes of assault, sex, theft and damage, arrears and debts, and substandard hygiene. But would authority intervention for some or even all of these reasons necessarily correlate with being a cause of trouble to others living around them? Amos did not investigate the incidence of this factor. In other words if we used the term 'problem families' to mean families requiring multiple agency intervention, would we be at one and the same time be identifying those families of which neighbours complained so bitterly?

Certainly there was an overlap. Some of the families who caused suffering to those living nearby had had lifelong social services and police involvement. For example the Sands family had lived in a row of nine terraced houses looking out over a green and recreation ground for twenty one years. The other houses had been occupied by similar families and all the children had grown up together. Mr. and Mrs. Sands however still had a seven year old daughter at home although their other children had left. They had been one of the first tenants, eight years earlier, to decide to buy their council house and since then they had put in double glazing, central heating and other individual touches to the house. All the neighbours had got on well together and helped each other out with car repairs, babysitting etc. Then two years earlier the Sands' next door neighbours had moved and a young single mother of two small children had been placed there by the council. At first Mrs. Sands had been sympathetic towards the girl. She had taken Pat and the children in one night after a row with her boyfriend. But things soon went sour. There was the awful noise. There were continual rows, banging of doors, Pat screaming at the children, all made worse by the fact that there were no carpets in the house and by the customary routine of Pat's household to be up in the night and sleep through the mornings. There was the rubbish. The garden had been left in a beautiful condition according to Mrs. Sands but Pat used it as a dustbin and just threw all her refuse and rubbish out there where it smelt and blew around. There was the language. Mrs. Sands said:

> I try to keep Sally (their seven year old daughter) away, but when Pat's children are in the garden you can't help hearing her effing and blinding at the kids.

Several of the neighbours had tried to do something about the situation. When reasonable complaints were met with abuse and no improvement ensued one neighbour had been to the council offices. He was told that yes, they knew Pat was a problem, in fact they had had to move her from a house in Claytown for the same reasons, but they had thought that putting her in such a nice respectable row of houses might set her an example and improve her habits. In fact Pat probably saw her neighbours as yet another set of hostile people trying to tell her what to do and push her around. She had reacted by showing them she did not care and could be as antisocial as she wanted. Whatever the psychology of the situation it was clear that the advent of Pat's household had worsened the quality of life for the tenants and owner occupiers of the terrace and did not seem to have helped Pat either. Mrs. Sands said it had made her bitter about the council:

They shouldn't have dumped her next door on us.
When the other family moved out the council man said
he'd never seen a house left so beautifully
decorated and clean. You should see it now, you
really should.

The misfortune of the Kent family was even greater.
Mr. and Mrs. Kent had been in bed and breakfast
accommodation and with a baby on the way had been desperate
for a house. They had not wanted to live on Omega but it
was the first vacancy offered. They soon discovered they
had been housed opposite one of the notorious families on
the estate, a family with four sons in their teens and
twenties, all of whom had court records and periods in local
authority residential homes, detention centres or borstals.
The father also had a prison record. The family kept a
number of Alsatian dogs. In the two years Mr. and Mrs. Kent
had lived in the house this family had broken one of their
windows, smashed tiles on their roof, set the dogs on them,
and terrorised them with rows and fights in the street. The
Kents had been advised by the police to take the family to
court over the broken tiles which they did and the family
was fined. Repercussions followed:

> Now every time we go out they shout obscenities at
> us, call us bastards and scroungers. But ever since
> we've been here there's been trouble because of
> them. The previous family left because of them, and
> their next door neighbour is terrified. The old
> lady who used to live next to them had to go into
> the mental hospital with her nerves because of them.
> When the police come they set their Alsatian dogs on
> the cops. The parents are as bad as the sons.
> Another neighbour said the people in the street
> tried to get up a petition to get them moved out but
> nothing ever came of it.

Mr. and Mrs. Kent's strategy was to keep their heads low:

> Now it's dark we don't go out hardly. The police
> are always up and down this way, and coming to the
> street fights, but we just keep indoors.

But not all 'problem' neighbours were of this type. For
example the Arthur family was woken each morning at dawn by
geese kept in a garden of a nearby house and a group of
neighbours had written to the council complaining about it.
Mr. and Mrs. Snape had West Indian neighbours who enjoyed
having riotous parties for their friends with music blaring
through open windows until the early hours but who in other

58

respects were conforming people. As Mr. Snape said:

> We had to call the police, it was about 2 a.m., we
> asked them to stop, but then called the police, they
> had to knock on the window to make themselves heard
> but then they did turn down the music. They're good
> neighbours otherwise but they do have these very
> loud noisy parties.

Mr. and Mrs. Nokes were upset because the house next door
adjoining theirs was dilapidated, dirty and the garden
looked like:

> Steptoes' rag and bone yard. I can't stand it and I
> can't see any reason for it. They're decent people
> or we wouldn't stay here at all if they were that
> bad, but the state of the place! All of us round
> here say we'd put a flag up if they moved. They did
> get reported to the council and I got accused of it
> but I didn't do it. They ought to have inspections
> of the houses, but they don't do that now.

One household caused such bad feeling over such a wide
area of the estate that a court case was brought. The
Higgins family lived opposite a small layby adjacent to a
corner house. The man in this corner house had knocked down
his front wall and concreted over the small front garden to
make hardstanding. On this were parked three rusty broken
cars and in the layby seven more. The back garden was like
a scrap yard of bits of cars and engines and wheels. It
seemed pretty plain that this man was running some kind of
repair business and sounds of welding and panel beating over
the evenings and weekends were another source of nuisance.
Mr. and Mrs. Higgins were of the opinion that the business
was not only against the terms of the council tenancy but
worse, was of a dubious nature, since cars appeared
overnight on the layby, often without tax, and they felt
that they could well be stolen. They had telephoned the
police a number of times about the cars. But the chief
objection and that of all the neighbours in the locality was
the junk yard and scrap heap appearance the rusty
dilapidated cars gave to the residential street. Many
families had written several times to the council.
Mr. Higgins had appealed to a local councillor. All the
neighbours in the vicinity had signed a petition. Finally
the council had been prodded into taking the man to court
for misuse of council property. Five neighbours had
attended as witnesses. The man's defence was that it was
not a business and he did not get paid for doing up the
cars, an extremely unlikely story but apparently one which

could not be proved either way. To everyone's surprise and dismay the council lost the case and had to pay costs. Mr. and Mrs. Higgins were distressed and furious since they had just begun to buy their house and said they would not have done so had they not been certain the council would eventually evict the man. To their further dismay they had recently learned that the cause of their anger was also now buying his house so the council's powers over his activities would be further limited.

From the above examples it was clear that all troublesome neighbours were not problem families though some were. And in reverse there were some families who would be regarded as problem families by social services and other agencies but who did not apparently cause trouble in their neighbourhood. For example Mr. and Mrs. Ellison lived next door to what would be a problem family to the authorities, but who did not cause the Ellisons any bother since the time they decided to have nothing to do with the family:

> The father is in and out of prison and she uses it as a red light area. The little girl wasn't being looked after properly and we were worried she was maybe being battered and not fed. We spoke to the health visitor who got in touch with next door's social worker. She calls every week but we don't know exactly what took place as we don't talk to next door.

Their decision to ignore the neighbours had been a result of one particular experience:

> When we first moved here we felt sorry for next door but she abused our friendship so we don't speak to her now. We left our cat with her when we went on holiday and it was starved when we came back. She never fed it once.

The case of Ms. Field was another example. Ms. Field's family had been on the longterm caseload of social services at least since she had been a small child. She and her sister had spent periods in care. At the time of the interview, the researcher felt that the two year old child was only minimally cared for and Ms. Field complained her daughter was always getting out of the flat and wandering off. The police had brought the child back each time alerted by someone on the estate who had telephoned them. Ms. Field and her sister had been involved in a drugs case and she was also on probation for stealing a pushchair. Nevertheless there was no evidence that Ms. Field was any problem to the other residents of the block of flats where she and her daughter lived.

Thus while residents with troublesome neighbours might refer to them as problem families as did Mr. Little there was plenty of evidence that there was no necessary connection between being a problem family (in the sense of requiring multiple agency intervention) and being a thorough nuisance to the neighbours. Another term was therefore required to refer to those families or persons who specifically caused annoyance, inconvenience, property damage, even fear and suffering, to those living around them. The term 'antisocial' seemed appropriate since this directly implied that very lack of awareness of, or lack of concern for, the consequences of their behaviour on others, which characterised the troublesome neighbours referred to by the residents interviewed.

In the study by Popplestone and Paris (1979) on the same topic the authors used the term 'difficult tenants' because they 'give rise to difficulties' for the housing departments through the complaints received by other tenants. Popplestone and Paris' definition is from the standpoint of the housing department while the definition used in this chapter is from the standpoint of the other residents.

Most of this chapter is concerned with communicating the misery, inconvenience and often fear produced in ordinary residents when they found themselves living close to difficult or antisocial families.

It may however be valuable at this point to give an account of what life was like for one of those antisocial families everyone else complained about. Mrs. Riley said:

All the neighbours hate us and we hate all the neighbours.

Mr. Riley had been in prison on three occasions for violent assaults, and on another occasion it had been for a series of robberies and thefts he did not admit to. His hot temper and liability to provocation by anything he regarded as a slight to him had led him to be involved in punch-ups in the local pub. He had a continuing feud with his brother who came round one night to his door with a chain threatening to 'do' him or else get his wife and kids. Mr. Riley leapt to the defence with a knife and when the police came he was the one to be arrested and prosecuted which he felt bitter about:

I'll always fight in self-defence or to settle an issue.

61

A number of incidents with neighbours had clearly been a consequence of putting this policy into practice in spite of his casting himself always in the role of victim. For example when their dog was in a fight with the 'vicious' dog of a neighbour Mr. Riley went round and told his neighbour plainly that if it happened again he personally would kill the neighbour's vicious dog. The Riley children played on the unfenced grass round the block of flats where the family lived and another family opposite apparently hit on the strategy of keeping the balls which frequently landed in their garden. Mr. Riley set off to retrieve a ball and 'asked' for it back. The ensuing exchange must have been less than polite for the other family called the police and accused Mr. Riley of, among other things, threatening to throw a cricket bat through their window. Another source of conflict was that, according to Mrs. Riley, they were the only family with young children in the block of twelve flats. On the ground floor there were elderly folk and in the rest were families with older children. Whether outdoors or indoors, it was inevitable that the three youngsters were going to cause noise and nuisance to those with a quieter lifestyle.

Thus a picture emerged of the Riley family as the neighbours must have seen them, noisy, with annoying children and an uncontrolled roaming dog, the constant source of rows and intimidating physical threats to anyone who made a complaint, and from time to time the cause of brawls and fights to which the police had to be called; on top of which Mr. Riley was no doubt seen as lowering the tone of the neighbourhood by being chronically unemployed and having a prison record. But the case of the Rileys also allowed a glimpse of how things appeared from the viewpoint of a family experiencing neighbourhood disapproval. They felt hated and victimised and responded by directing hate and suspicion to everyone on the estate and all the agencies they were involved with as well. They also had a strong desire to leave the estate. Mr. Riley giving as his reason that:

> I don't like the type of family living here. The children are picking up bad language from the other children.

Yet he himself had been born and brought up on the estate. Mr. Riley was always phoning the police to complain about other people's transgressions. When cars were parked on the grass outside the flats he called the police but they never came which he interpreted as a personal slight to himself.

He lost a job after two days and reckoned the boss:

> had been blackmailed by my enemies.

Mrs. Riley also felt the family was discriminated against on all sides. She had asked the health visitor to try to get a place for the four year old in a special nursery. She had not heard any more yet she knew of families with only two children who had been helped in this way. She said the doctor was just as bad. He had been called in the night to their one year old son, had not come till the morning, and as a result of his neglect the baby had had to be admitted to hospital with pneumonia. The family did not use any leisure facilities on the estate for, as Mrs. Riley said about the community centre:

> There's no point in going there to meet people from the estate who don't like us and who we don't want to know.

The story of the Rileys exemplified some of the factors over and above the pathology or aggressive antisocial lifestyle of the culprits which might have contributed to the frequency of neighbour troubles on Omega estate. One of these factors was the mixing of generations. This factor was exemplified in the case of Mr. Little. In his case the placing of a row of flats for the elderly below a row of family maisonettes was clearly a precipitating factor in the troubles. Mr. Little had had constant nuisance from his upstairs neighbours:

> The man never works, he's an alcoholic. The oldest boy has a very noisy motorcycle. But last winter was awful. One of the sons had an air rifle, he was firing it out of the window at the sheds. I went to his mother and spoke to the son but got no satisfaction. So I went to the police and it didn't happen any more but they knew it was me that had reported it. They emptied dustbins into my garden, they pulled up all my rosebushes, and put stink bombs through my letterbox. I phoned the police again but then I got a solicitor's letter from the boy's mother saying I mustn't accuse the boy without proof. I've heard no more, but everybody else complained about the shooting and I was the only one who did something about it and so I was penalised.

Mrs. Ouseley, a retired divorced lady, lived in an extensive complex of blocks of small flats which was owned by a housing association but with the housing department sharing the tenant nomination rights. The result was that numerous young couples and young families who were not yet eligible for allocation to a council house or maisonette would get a flat there until such time as they could hope to accumulate points for a transfer. But in addition there were single elderly folk who had been allocated a flat on priority and who saw the flats as a permanent home. They were frequently placed in the ground floor flats. Mrs. Ouseley resented the transient population of young families:

> It's no good here for an elderly person because there's too many children. We should be separate from children. But there's no garden, just public space and all the kids run riot. There's no peace for anybody old. They should put all the families together away from the elderly people. It's more of a recreation ground for kids than a garden for people's homes; all the mothers sit outside my windows in the summer and I can't hear the TV. They shouldn't mix old and young. I will ask for a transfer or put in for an exchange if it doesn't improve. Not getting peace in your own home is very bad.

Mrs. Berg, a seventy seven year old widow, lived in a block of flats in a cul de sac of mainly family houses. She too lived on the ground floor, her large front window only a few feet from a low fence separating grass from pavement. She complained that:

> The dogs all get in and people leave rubbish and children peer in and bang on the window or throw stones.

Often there was a crowd of boys and girls sitting on her little fence and she was unable to hear the television. She had sometimes gone out to complain of the noise to them and:

> They called me an old cow.

Possibly as a sequel to her grumbles she had had 'human muck' pushed through her letter box and, on a further occasion, blue paint sprayed over her front door. She had called the police on these occasions and on the second one the police had brought the boy responsible with his father along to her flat to apologise. The general noise and harassment however continued and Mrs. Berg was of the opinion like Mrs. Ouseley that:

> They shouldn't mix old and young.

She was also disturbed by a family with two babies living above her flat:

> You can hear them going to the toilet and the toys

on the floor make an awful noise.

Mr. Little, Mrs. Berg and Mrs. Ouseley were typical complainants of the annoyance caused to the elderly by the activities of numerous children close by. But two other elderly widows had a favourable attitude to living among families. Mrs. Knight, a resident of nineteen years in her flat, and who had her sons' families living on the estate, said that Omega was a wonderful place for old people. Mrs. Austin, a resident of even longer standing than Mrs. Knight, who had been in her bungalow for twenty one years and who also had her son and her daughter living with their families on the estate gave what might be a clue. She said she liked to see people, especially the children, walking about on the street:

> They never do me any harm. I think the kids treat you alright if you treat them alright. Mr. Morley (her widower neighbour) is always shouting at them. They only have to sit on his front wall for him to rush out at them. Well, he gets called names. He asks for trouble.

These two ladies were benefitting rather than suffering from the mixing of the generations. The difference could be the length of time they had lived there or the presence of their children and grandchildren on the estate, a factor which itself might have affected their attitude to young people. There could be another significant difference too, related to housing design, for Mrs. Knight lived in a block of flats set back from the road with a concealed entrance and Mrs. Austin lived in her own bungalow with a front garden, while the other old people mentioned lived in ground floor flats with windows looking on to public space.

Another factor therefore which might have had a bearing on the incidence of neighbour trouble on Omega was the design and structure of the housing. This possibility was worth exploring further. The Donaldsons, for example, lived in a terrace next door to an infamous family of four wild children and an alcoholic woman with a succession of alcoholic cohabitees. The children, when they were not in local authority care, were left on their own for days and would cause fights, trample across gardens and steal food. When the mother was in things were even worse for Mrs. Donaldson although quite why she was so afraid was not clear:

> She got me in such a state I'm on pills from the doctor. I couldn't even go out the back to hang the washing out, I was so afraid. They drink too much.

She never says a word if she's sober only when she's
been drinking. My nerves are shattered. You never
know when she'll start up again and then I'll be a
bag of nerves for days.

It seemed that it was not being able to get away from the
sight, the sounds and the face to face confrontations with
the antisocial neighbours that so oppressed Mrs. Donaldson.
Things would have never got to such a pitch if the next door
neighbours had lived in a separate house rather than a
terrace, or if the walls between the houses had been thick
and insulated. Mr. Donaldson said:

This house was not built, it was just chucked up.
The walls are so thin you can hear every little
noise.

If there had been a solid five foot wall between the gardens
the Donaldsons' garden fence would not have broken down and
Mrs. Donaldson would not have been so exposed to her
neighbour's drunken abuse when she went to hang out the
washing. Exactly the same applied to the case of Mr. and
Mrs. Sands. Pat's banging, stomping, rowing, swearing and
using the garden as a dustbin would not have been so
upsettingly audible and visible within a solid house
enclosed by a substantial wall. A good deal of the
hostility provoked by the Riley family would never have
happened if they had been in their own house, with a garden
to contain the children and the dog. The widespread problem
of local children vandalising cars could have been prevented
by the increased provision of lock up garages, the cause of
constant grouse on Omega, where the few garages which
existed were in blocks at a distance from the dwellings and
which had to be separately applied for and rented. The vast
majority of residents had to park in the road out of
necessity.

There were numerous other examples of neighbour problems
where a contributory factor was some aspect of the physical
structure or layout of the housing. The obvious invitation
to children (or an angry adult) of the upper maisonette
balcony which overhung the tiny private garden of the
dwelling below was mentioned in the case of Mr. Little.
Ms. Drew in a ground floor maisonette had the same problem:

I don't like living in a maisonette. The kids have
nothing to do, especially in the holidays, and the
ones above spit, and throw things into the garden
from the balcony. I can't let Darryl play out
there. We get bottles and all sorts. They're just
out to annoy people because there's nothing else to

do.

The nuisance and conflict caused by children using the public unfenced grass space round flats and maisonettes and at the ends of closes and cul de sacs have already been mentioned (see for example the case of 'Sid' in Chapter 2). Even where there was fencing it was vulnerable and a source of trouble. A number of respondents such as the Donaldsons had trouble from neighbours' children partly due to the flimsiness of fencing. People who lived on ends of rows or corners found their gardens were used as thoroughfares or extensions to wasteland play areas. Ms. Redder said:

> The boys jump from the garages over the fence at the back. I've neglected the garden because the kids broke the fences and run all over it. They give you a lot of cheek if you say anything. We're most affected because we're the end house but I've heard other neighbours out shouting.

The likely connection between housing design and layout and some kinds of neighbour trouble was made explicit by a number of respondents. Mr. Brown after expressing disapproval of his next door neighbours' activities said:

> The way they build these council estates makes it worse, the fences are so low and there's no privacy.

Some people indicated that they would not like to live in the newer part of the estate which was built in the second phase in the midsixties. Mrs. Sawyer said:

> It's too closed in, no spaces at the back. I know people that lived there and they said it's bad, neighbour trouble I mean.

And Mr. Sawyer said:

> If you put people in flats, or in houses all close together, you'll get trouble. The houses on the estate are all compact and then there's great big open spaces, it's not sensible.

Mr. Arthur referred to the same area, and said:

> Some of the houses are built just the way they encourage people to fight with each other, all packed together.

Mrs. Mulpepper put the same point clearly when she commented:

> They put you all so close together yet it's a big estate. I can't explain it. My neighbours are

67

friendly and yet it's not a friendly place. I think
it's because we're all so close together that
there's always somebody doing something to annoy
you, if it's only music, or lighting a bonfire or
mending a car, it's because we're all packed
together.

And Mr. Aston, who lived in the newer part said:

This estate is no use to live in. All the flats
should be blown up. The houses are too highdensity.
There's no proper fences or walls. They should
build houses like they used to - semis with proper
gardens back and front and proper walls or hedges.

These observations were interesting because they confirmed
some statistical findings of the research. These were in
brief that resident satisfaction was significantly higher in
the western half of the estate where eighty three per cent
of respondents were happy with their neighbourhood than in
the eastern half where only fifty three per cent said they
were happy. Frequency of neighbour trouble followed the
same pattern with sixty per cent of those living in the
newer half reporting current or recent trouble compared with
forty seven per cent of those living in the older half. One
contributory factor to this difference could be that the
residents who got on well with all their neighbours were
those who had lived there longest and there were more
longterm residents in the western half. But of course the
longstanding residents were those who had elected to remain.
In general those in the western half were more satisfied and
got on better with neighbours than those in the eastern half
irrespective of length of residence and irrespective of
whether they lived in a house or flat. The eastern half had
been built in the second phase and to a higher density than
the original development. Seventy per cent of the flats and
maisonettes lay in the newer half. (Interestingly Omega had
a higher proportion of maisonettes, eight per cent of the
dwellings, than any other estate; Chalkbury however had a
much higher proportion of flats, over half the dwellings).

There certainly seemed to be reason to take seriously the
idea that the provision of high density forms of housing,
with little or no sound insulation, with inadequate and
insubstantial fencing round gardens, and the existence of
public patches of grass round flats and maisonettes (all
features more typical of the eastern rather than the western
half) were physical factors which precipitated and
exacerbated neighbour trouble.

Let us now look at what options were available to people when faced with trouble from neighbours. Calling the police was the measure most frequently resorted to, whenever matters reached a crisis, an outright conflict, or real damage had been sustained. The police were called in thirty five per cent of neighbour incidents and at one time or another by forty one per cent of those with neighbour trouble. For example, Mr. Morgan and other residents in his row were quite accustomed to calling the police to come and deal with their neighbours:

> The police have been called out so many times now, that it's no longer just our word against theirs, they know that we're all getting cheesed off with them.

Over the preceding year Mr. Morgan had called them on acount of a missing bike which he said the son of the troublesome family had stolen, for a break-in and robbery by the same person (which came to court), and when they could hear the husband beating his wife. Mr. and Mrs. Kent resorted to the police but only when they were actually under attack from their neighbours opposite, with blocks of wood smashing their roof tiles. Similarly Mr. and Mrs. Trapp called the police when a gang of neighbours' children:

> were shouting at my kids and throwing dustbin lids at the door.

Many persons attempted some direct action in the form of complaints or threats before resorting to calling out the police. Thus the Snapes when their party loving neighbours were still disturbing the peace after midnight, first went round to make a complaint and when that had no effect, called the police at 2 a.m. Mr. and Mrs. Hilsden and other neighbours had been troubled by the noise, fights, and vandalism continually being caused by a large family of children living opposite. When they actually damaged the front fence Mr. Hilsden went over to see the mother and lodge a complaint. According to him:

> She did a war dance and later came across waving a bread knife.

He then contacted the police but apparently:

> The sergeant said there wasn't much they could do.

The Misses Naylor suffered from children throwing stones, damaging the car so that it had to be resprayed and trampling plants in the front garden. One of them went to see the mother who in fact dragged one of the children around to apologise. But the vandalism continued. The next time when one sister caught a lad in the act of throwing stones at the car she 'clouted' him. When this did not work either, they contacted the police only to be told there was nothing they could do because the children involved were under ten years old. Mr. Cope said that:

> This woman was hitting her child with a strap outside on the grass. I went over and told her to leave it alone. You can imagine the kind of things she said. So I called the police but they didn't do anything. She just shut the door in their face.

When Mr. Little got no satisfaction after complaining to the family with the airgun, he went to the police who investigated thoroughly and as a result Mr. Little suffered reprisals from the family. He was clearly seen as interfering in what was not his business and this attitude came through from some other respondents' experiences. Mrs. Jordan recounted how a woman living nearby:

> was getting kicked to death but we were the only ones who would ring the police. The neighbours were all watching but nobody would ring the police. You're supposed to help your neighbours but if you do they say you're nosey and interfering. I thought the idea was to get the police to help sort things out but nobody else does.

Whatever Mrs. Jordan felt about the reaction of her neighbours, the fact remained that the police did get called to a very high proportion of neighbour disturbances.

Taking up the cudgels oneself in fact rarely worked either. Several respondents, having tried remonstrating with those causing trouble, and having failed, never took further action at all, but kept their heads down waiting for things to get better which eventually they usually did. Ms. Redder said:

> We've had 'Wogs Go Home' written on the wall. I never did anything just talk to them and ask them to go. But they're a bit older now and don't do it any more.

Mr. and Mrs. Newson said:

> The kids drove us mad, the next door neighbour mad and the man across the road mad by constant banging on the garages. We spoke to the parents but they said 'You don't own the close, you can't stop them', but there's two lots and I think the bigger ones have scared off the younger ones now.

Only one indomitable old lady, Mrs. Day, claimed success for her independent measures:

> When I first moved here two years ago, the teenagers caused trouble in the passageway, smoking, rowdy, banging on the doors, everything to annoy you. I threw a bucket of water over them and one lad threatened me with a carving knife. I didn't call the police because they're useless. If they don't witness it they don't do anything. But on bonfire night I gave them (the kids) some old wood from the shed and they've been alright since. A few kind words, I expect.

A surprisingly high proportion, a third, of people with neighbour trouble had not done anything at all about the nuisance. As Ms. Drew said:

> You can't do anything about kids without causing trouble with the neighbours, can you?

The same sentiments were reflected by Mrs. Staines:

> The kids are all over our wall. I don't say anything for fear of their parents. You have to be very careful if you say anything to the kids, it goes straight to the parents. They take offence, get snotty if you say anything.

Mrs. Lane had worse problems. There were three families in the road who were not very pleasant to live near:

> They're not clean, houses and gardens in a mess, rubbish strewn about, the kids steal milk and last time we went away we had our front door smashed in. We can't leave the house to go on holiday now, because of the vandalism.

But neither the Lanes nor other aggrieved neighbours had ever done anything:

> No. We accept that if we complained it would only get worse. Or if we told the authorities, and they found out, there'd be repercussions. It's best to lie low and ignore it.

The other reason for not doing anything was the feeling that it was hopeless, nothing would improve. As Mrs. Jordan said:

> We tend to let it go. Tried shouting once but got a lot of abuse back so what's the use?

Ms. Worral said exactly the same:

If you say anything to them they give you a mouthful
so it's really a waste of time.

There were other methods mentioned by some respondents of
dealing with trouble caused by neighbours among which one
could be termed 'preventative measures'. One young couple
for example, the Liffeys, found that the people before them
had moved mainly due to:

teenagers always hanging round on bikes, making
noise and nuisance.

The Liffeys had inherited a back garden:

like a POW camp, to try to keep the teenagers out.

Mrs. Berg sat in the dark in her living room which looked
out on the pavement and then before she put on any lights
she pulled across thick heavy curtains and checked for
cracks. She also had an extra bolt on her front door.
Mr. Aston asked the police to keep an eye on his house if he
was going away for more than a day. The police evidently
took such requests seriously for on one occasion Mr. Aston
found himself challenged on his own property by a policeman
who had not yet received information from the police station
that Mr. Aston had returned. The Lanes said they no longer
felt they could leave the house to go on holiday. The Kents
and Mrs. Donaldson, who both had almost daily harassment
from antisocial and aggressive neighbours, virtually
imprisoned themselves in their houses after dark. Mr. and
Mrs. Ellison and Mr. and Mrs. Sands, both of whom had
difficult families living directly next door in a terraced
house or maisonette, deliberately minimised contact and
never spoke to their neighbours. According to Mr. Dale
there were two families who had already been moved around
the estate for causing trouble, and were still causing it,
and:

No-one likes them and no-one speaks to them.

This explicit neighbourhood disapproval was also shown when
Mrs. Berry stated that a particular family which caused
trouble in the road, was the only family not invited to
communal street parties and outings which she helped to
organise.

The ultimate resort of residents plagued by antisocial
neighbours however was the housing department to whom one
could lodge complaints individually or through a councillor
or else get together with others to present a petition for
the removal of the troublesome family. Twenty two per cent
of respondents with neighbour trouble had contacted the

housing department in one of these ways. The type of neighbour problem for which housing department intervention was seen as the way out was of a different kind than the crises (late night party, assaults or teenage intimidation or vandalism) for which the police were routinely called. People seemed to call on the council when a particular family could be clearly identified as the longstanding source of conflict, delinquency or nuisance; a question of an antisocial lifestyle rather than occasional incidents. A typical year's petitions from the estate to the council included the following concerns: late night noise; noise from amplified electric guitar; noise from continuous domestic violence; too many noisy late night visitors; family accused of being a fire risk; noise from CB radio; family accused of throwing rubbish all over garden; noisy dogs. Nearly all were examples of audible or visual affront. Thus the Berrys and other neighbours wrote to the housing department about the family excluded from the street activities. The Donaldsons had been to see their councillor and they and others had written to the council hoping to get their drunken and abusive neighbours removed; they had also put themselves on the transfer list. (In the event fate stepped in and the Donaldsons' plaguey neighbours accidentally burnt their own house down so had to be removed to accommodation elsewhere). Mr. Enworthy had written frequently to the council about a family who were very noisy both on the stairs and passages and in the flat in one of the tower blocks. They apparently:

had no carpets and held continuous parties.

He said he thought the council had written to the family responsible and as a result they had 'quietened down'. There was no doubt that the housing department did take notice when complaints poured in about some particular antisocial household and petitions always came up before the monthly housing management subcommittee for consideration. But ultimately all they could do was to rehouse the family elsewhere and wait for the cycle to begin again. Thus the outraged neighbours living in Mr. and Mrs. Sands' terrace had been told by the council that they knew Pat was a problem, they had already had to move her from Claytown, but they had hoped that the example of the respectable row of residents would improve her standards. Mr. Dale had a similar story no doubt exaggerated but probably seen the same way by other neighbours around:

They dumped two single mothers who got thrown out of Claytown up by the school and then they got thrown out of there, now they're next door to each other

> again, at the end here. They ran a prostitution
> racket. You could see the boys queuing up. The
> police kept coming and the neighbours got up a
> petition and they've quietened down now.

These were the families Mr. Dale had said no-one spoke to.
A number of success stories resulting in the disliked
antisocial family being moved on, were claimed by
respondents. Mr. and Mrs. Rawlings had had a large and
noisy family of unsupervised and aggressive children living
close by who apparently terrorised other local children
including their son. Mrs. Rawlings and others had been to
the housing department to try to get the family moved. It
seemed that the family themselves wanted a transfer to
Claytown in any case. One way or another it happened that
the 'council lady' (she might have meant rent collector,
housing visitor or even a social worker) was present at the
very time that the mother of the antisocial family burst in
to the Rawlings and attacked Mrs. Rawlings, accusing their
son of hitting her daughter:

> The council lady took me upstairs and phoned the
> police. The police took Mrs. P. back home. They
> were moved the next week.

The witnessing of the crisis by the 'council lady' was
probably a precipitating factor in expediting the transfer
of the antisocial family. The Hilsdens had finally got rid
of the similarly troublesome family causing havoc in their
street when the woman who had done 'a war dance' allegedly
stabbed her husband in a dispute and the neighbours got up a
petition. They were moved soon after to another part of the
estate. Similarly the woman complained of by the Copes was
removed:

> The neighbours got up a petition together and they
> took one of her children away. They went and gave
> her a new house in the end.

The petition lodged by the Higgins family and a large number
of neighbours against the man with the business in rusty
cars of dubious origins had succeeded only in forcing the
council to take civil action against the man for misuse of
the premises which, as was related above, had unexpectedly
failed. Since the man had by then begun to buy his house
there was very little the council could do to alleviate the
discord. In the case of the infamous family housed opposite
the Kents, it seemed a petition had been sent to the council
in the past but no action taken. The family had been in the
same house for twenty years causing trouble to neighbours
and to the various authorities the whole time. But somehow
they had made that part of the estate their territory and

the response of some of those living around them seemed to be resignation to a life of tranquillisers, periods in a mental hospital for relief, lying low and waiting for a transfer. One researcher heard a social worker once comment about the family that:

> the only place to put them would be in the middle of a large field with an eight foot wall around them.

The above remark though flippant served to raise the question of what would be the best policy to deal with the problem of incorrigible antisocial families since the council's supply of houses surrounded by high walls situated in the middle of large fields was limited. The question was also raised as to what extent neighbour disputes and clashes of lifestyle were the responsibility of the housing department. As the illustrations and examples indicate, the department was the only resort for people whose lives were made a misery on a longterm basis by the behaviour of neighbours. Intervention by other agencies could help at crisis points but where the conflict was one of totally incompatible lifestyles the only solution was for one or other party to the trouble to move away. There has been an increasing move towards expanding the responsibility of housing departments for tenant welfare and by introducing tenants' agreements which detail specific obligations on both sides. Moreover it must be borne in mind that any housing department has a common law obligation (in common with any landlord) of 'ensuring the tenant's peaceful enjoyment of the dwelling' (Housing Research Group 1981). Add to this the evidence already given that council planning and allocation policies and especially the structure, design and layout of the housing sometimes precipitates and commonly aggravates neighbour incompatibilities then clearly the council does have a responsibility for sorting things out. Popplestone and Paris (1979) made one of these points:

> And yet, the public sector has put up housing of a kind that makes extreme demands upon its occupiers, even when it is well built. And budgetary restraints and architectural experimenting, together, mean that much of this housing is not well built.

The Housing Research Group were alive to this issue too:

> Poor internal noise insulation, costly and inefficient heating systems and high condensation are just three examples of major problems which thousands of tenants have suffered in recently built estates in the name of keeping down building costs.

And such weaknesses in the quality of dwellings do not just have a marginal effect on tenants and staff; in extreme cases they are major factors in the creation of hostile and unmanageable housing.

Because of these responsibilities, i.e. the responsibility of the council for the conditions which breed unsatisfactory social environments in the first place, and the departments' ability to provide the only solutions which can bring relief from suffering to the tenants to whom they have an obligation, the onus of preventing, minimising or alleviating troubles between neighbours clearly is on the local authority housing department. And this is particularly important on problem estates such as Omega.

6 Law and order

Omega residents as was shown in Chapter 3 called out the police at a rate higher than elsewhere. They reported offences committed against them as victims, offences they suspected of being committed against others, vandalism against property and a very wide range of other incidents such as street fighting, pub brawls and domestic disputes; complaints about noise, mainly motorcycles; reports of accidents; reports of suspicious or peculiar behaviour; reports about missing or disruptive children; complaints about cars parked on grass or across exits; and a miscellany of other occurrences such as a bird up a chimney, getting locked out of the house, finding a purse, a heart attack, and requests for the police to keep an eye on property.

And again the question has to be asked, was there really more crime on Omega, were there really more incidents so threatening the public order that the police were required? Or were there other factors which simply made it more likely than any disquieting event would be reported rather than dealt with locally? The chapter on neighbour troubles indicated very little in the way of community social control or community tolerance on Omega. And so it seemed was the case with the more general issues of law and order.

Some predisposing factors have already become evident. The unpopular maisonettes (of which there were more on Omega than anywhere else) and a particular type of square built block of flats seemed to attract trouble and make all goings on into a visible and audible nuisance by the way that they were designed with overhanging balconies, lack of sound insulation, communal doors and stairways, windows looking directly onto public grass or pavement etc. Another factor which will be discussed in more detail in the next chapter was the sheer number of teenagers living on the estate, a concentration much greater than anywhere else in the city. Over a quarter of the Omega population according to the 1981 census were in the age group ten to nineteen years. And of course the rate of convicted offenders living on Omega was higher than for other areas although great care must be taken before assuming that this necessarily reflected a greater criminality of the Omega population.

In investigating the experience of and attitude of Omega residents to questions of law and order let us look first at the kinds of offences they complained of, what other incidents they called the police for, and what they thought of, indeed expected of, the police force in their area.

Fifty five per cent of householders interviewed said they had themselves been victims of one or more offences over the previous two years. The probability of having been a victim seemed to be higher in the higher density eastern part of the estate where sixty four per cent of householders interviewed complained of offences compared with forty five per cent of those in the west. However the picture was made clearer when the offences suffered were divided into two categories. There were offences of criminal damage and vandalism such as stones through windows, damage to car tyres, aerials, mirrors etc., wrecked clothes drying trees, paint sprayed on doors and so on, which could broadly speaking be classed as opportunistic. A greater degree of premeditation and specificity of target distinguished the other category of offences such as car or bicycle thefts, meter break-ins, burglaries or assaults. Sixty per cent of the offences complained of in interviews were in the first category. This criminal damage and vandalism was much higher in the eastern part; the victims lived predominantly in flats or maisonettes; and less than half the incidents were reported to police. The more serious crimes were equally spread out across the estate but, rather unexpectedly, over eighty per cent had been inflicted on residents in houses rather than flats and maisonettes. All but two of the fifty two crimes in this category had been reported to police.

The influence of the residential environment on victimisation seemed therefore fairly clear. The nuisance, harassment and aggravation fostered by the higher density housing of the eastern half resulted in a high rate of criminal damage and vandalism there, much of which there seemed little point in reporting to the police. On the other hand, houses, wherever they were on the estate, presented a safer target with less chance of surveillance or being surprised in the pursuance of break-ins, burglaries and deliberate thefts.

There was some evidence that social factors also contributed to the likelihood of victimisation, possibly as a reprisal. Families with children at home were more likely to complain of, and to report, offences against them than the elderly, single or childless persons.

Only six out of the fifty serious offences reported by householders interviewed had been solved in the sense of someone being charged or convicted. Two assaults resulted in prison sentences. Compensation was ordered in the criminal damage case referred to in Chapter 5 in which youths deliberately threw blocks of wood at, and smashed, the roof tiles of the Kent's house. Another conviction resulted from the case of Mr. and Mrs. Firth who had their house broken into while they were in bed. They realised afterwards that the burglar had taken the precaution of doping their dog. Money had been taken from the meters. The police had a suspect but it was only when he was caught redhanded in a subsequent and identical manoeuvre elsewhere that the police were able to prosecute. Mr. and Mrs. Firth had a favourable view of the police work on the crime. Their view contrasted with that of Mr. and Mrs. Morgan who lived near a family in which father and son were known to the law, the father having served a prison sentence. The son had stolen a bicycle belonging to the Morgans:

> He admitted taking it but said he'd put it back and he hadn't. The police did absolutely nothing.

However later the son burgled the Morgan's house taking medals and jewellery and causing damage. The youth had been prosecuted and convicted but Mr. Morgan still felt badly about the way he personally had been treated by the police and the court. For example:

> We went to court but it was put back two times because of other charges involved and we lost three days' wages. They said they'd compensate us but we never heard any more.

In spite of the fact that so few crimes reported by respondents had been cleared up two thirds of respondent victims felt the police had done the best they could be expected to, and that while this left them out of pocket and inconvenienced, they accepted this as one of life's trials. For example Mr. Prowting had suffered a burglary and the contents of the electricity meter were taken while he was away:

> The police did their best but in the end I had to pay because they couldn't find who did it.

Similarly Ms. Belling said:

> We got broken into last Christmas and called the police. They took all the particulars and were helpful but they caught no-one. So now the housing department say I've got to pay to replace the windows they broke when entering but I can't afford to.

All the stolen cars had been recovered by police but often with contents missing or having suffered damage. Mr. Lyle lost £200 worth of tools when his car was stolen. He felt the police had been helpful but had told him there was not much they could do to retrieve the tools even though Mr. Lyle claimed he knew who had stolen the car. Mr. Dale had had his car stolen from the road outside his house on five occasions in two years. Though the police always brought it back he had lost his spare wheel and on one occasion the car was dented and the clutch and cylinder were broken. For all these things he had to pay himself since presumably he was not covered by comprehensive insurance. As he was not the only one victimised in this way Mr. Dale felt the police must have a good idea who was responsible for the car thefts but he said that no charges were ever made against anyone. In desperation he fitted his car with an anti-thief chain on the wheel but the police advised against this as they said that the thief would simply saw through the wheel and he would have more damage to repair than if he just left it alone. At the time of the interview Mr. Dale said that he had worked out that it would be more economical to cycle to work and to sell his car (which he had done); he could hire one for weekends when the family wanted to go somewhere.

Unlike cars, bicycles were hardly ever found and returned by police. Mr. Wyatt was the only one ever to get a bike recovered but it was 'all broken up'. Most people shared the resigned attitude of Mr. King:

They've pinched my bike again. I've had seven bikes
stolen in the past eighteen months and got none of
them back. Yes, of course I phoned the police but
what can they do? I'll never get it back.

Similarly, Mr. Cutler who had had all his possessions stolen
from his car parked outside said:

I went to the police station and they were very
helpful, very satisfactory, but I got nothing back,
I didn't expect to see anything again.

The respondents quoted above were showing some understanding
of the difficulties facing the police in dealing with
frequent and petty property crimes in the area; and there
was a feeling underlying their remarks that a certain level
of crime had to be put up with in an area of dense housing
with a high teenage population.

A number of respondents did have grievances against the
police as a result of their experience. Mr. Morgan has
already been quoted. Mrs. Mulpepper was dismissive of
police effectiveness:

We had a break-in last week, they took some money.
They came through the window. We were all asleep in
bed at the time. We phoned from next door and a
panda came and they took fingerprints. Break-ins
happen all the time but a fat lot of good it does,
calling the police. You don't get it back anyway.
We won't bother if it happens again.

One frequent complaint about the police by those respondents
who had been victims of crime but felt negatively towards
the police was that the police took no action even though
the victim had been able to tell them who they believed,
even 'knew', was responsible. Already mentioned in this
regard was Mr. Lyle. Mr. Jordan complained:

You ring them up and they don't want to do anything,
like my daughter had some money taken from her
bedroom. We all knew who'd done it but the police
wouldn't do anything about it.

Another case was related by Mr. Nott:

A madman (I know who it was) drove his car straight
onto the grass patch outside and smashed up my car.
The police came and took details but nothing ever
happened. I had to pay for the damage myself.

Mr.Rawlings was annoyed at what he saw as a lack of action
in his case. He had had two attempted break-ins for which

the police had come:

But they're useless, they do nothing.

Mr. Rawlings had himself made enquiries and discovered, he claimed, the culprits but the police had apparently not followed it up.

One explanation of the perceived reluctance of local police to prosecute in these circumstances could have been the feeling that more harm than good would be done by bringing suspicions and hostilities out into the open this way; or they might have felt that where people in the same neighbourhood were accusing each other, that they were dealing more with internecine warfare than calculated criminal acts. One example supported the idea of a certain community cooling policy by the police in respect of disputes between neighbours. Ms. Bingham had had a whole side of new fencing, for which she herself had paid £60, stolen and burned on bonfire night by youths. She had phoned the police and two boys were found who owned up to the offence. The police made arrangements then with the boys' parents and Ms. Bingham for each of them to pay her £2 per week until she had £60. This seemed a very sensible way of solving the problem without the need to take the boys to court. However Ms. Bingham said:

I've had £2 from each of them so far and I don't think I'll ever the see the rest of it. One of them's mother is a single parent and she says she can't afford to pay it back but so am I and she should control her son.

The other common complaint was that having reported a crime to the police, the victim never heard any more about it and was left wondering if anything had been done to try to find the culprit, or if anyone would be punished. For example Ms. Madden had been impressed by how quickly the police had responded when she had disturbed burglars in her house in the night:

They were here in less than five minutes in a panda, then another in a van, then one with a dog.

She heard rumours that someone had been caught but:

We heard no more at all about it.

Similarly Mrs. Vernon said:

I was alone in the house in bed at night and there was a break-in and the meter was done. There were several done in the block that night. I called the police and they came and asked questions but I never saw or heard from them again.

And Mrs. Hawley's story was identical:

We had this break-in. The burglars did about twelve houses in that one night, all around here, and the police came and took fingerprints and that but I never knew if they got caught because they never came back to tell us anything.

Mr. and Mrs. Roper had found their son's bicycle all smashed up outside their house and the police had said they thought they knew who it was. However, said Mr. Roper:

That was a year ago and we never heard any more about it. We're very disenchanted about that. It was only six months old and cost us £100.

The Rowlands' son had been beaten up by another youth as he walked across the park and had returned home shaken and bruised. The police were called and came and photographed the injuries both immediately and again the following day. As the assailant was known the Rowlands assumed they would at least hear what had happened to him. As they heard nothing whatsoever they assumed the boy was 'let off' but they would have felt better if they had been informed of the situation by the police.

So it seemed that as with tenant-housing department relationships, lack of information could so easily be interpreted by residents as 'them' yet again simply not caring. Mr. Rawlings expressed this forcibly:

They do nothing. They just don't want to know about Omega.

In fact half the respondents expressed negative views on the efficiency of the police on the grounds of their not doing enough. This raised the question as to what the expectations of estate residents were of the police force. Most people had plenty of views when they were asked what they saw as the main job of the police. The most frequently expressed view was that their main job was deterrent patrolling, and well over half of these responses specified that the patrolling should be on foot. Respondents viewed as next in importance the maintenance of law and order; this included detecting crimes, catching thieves, recovering stolen property and dealing with vandals. Another duty of the police which was felt to be vital was responding to emergencies and coming quickly when called. A few respondents expressed the view that the police should also be concerned with making themselves acquainted with people and what was going on on the estate. As with other working class areas that have been studied (e.g. Davies, 1978; Mawby, 1979) there was no evidence of a widespread hostile attitude to the police. Eighty three per cent of respondents with an opinion wanted more police around the estate, only five per cent wanted fewer.

People's expectations of the police were actually very high. There was at the time just one regular beat policeman for Omega. He was a wellknown figure, friendly, to be seen around for part of every day. Panda cars cruised around on Friday and Saturday nights and they were also responsible for responding to calls made by residents to the station, reports, complaints and requests for help. The often confused and conflicting expectations by residents of the police can be shown by examining in closer detail some of the situations other than crimes committed in which respondents called the police. Some of the examples raised the question of to what extent the police should be regarded as all purpose keepers of the peace, and to what extent the residents of a neighbourhood (any neighbourhood, not just Omega) should be expected to deal with local troubles themselves. The Dowtys noticed a young man 'high on glue-sniffing' who was staggering about on the grass near their house and frightening the children playing there. Rather than asking the man where he lived, or asking the children or neighbours around if they knew who he was, the Dowtys called the police. Fifteen minutes later they arrived. The man was still there and the police took him away. In a similar case, the Rawlings saw:

> this blind drunk kid lying down on the grass outside.

They did not apparently approach him to see if he was alright or if he could tell them where he lived. They saw him through the window and telephoned the police. This being a Saturday night the police must have had their hands full with more serious matters because according to the Rawlings:

> no-one came at all. Two hours later the kid managed to get up and went off. He could have died, couldn't he, or been beaten up.

The implication was that the Rawlings felt the entire responsibility for the teenager's welfare rested with the police once they had alerted them. The McKellans heard screams outside their house one night, did not investigate but called the police. On this occasion the police came in force with two pandas and a policewoman in a van. Nothing and no-one was found. Mrs. Donaldson rang the police to tell them some children were fighting outside but no pandas arrived. Mr. Jordan was indignant at the police response when he reported to the police that his daughter had had some money taken from her bedroom by her friend:

> The police wouldn't do anything about it. They don't want to know. They could be doing a bloody sight more than they're doing now.

The Vernons had had rude words written over their front windows in lipstick on Halloween night. They had called the police and told them whom they felt sure it was that had done it:

> They were no use. They never even called on them.

Ms. Redder's problem with a bird stuck in the chimney was mentioned before; it was eventually sorted out by a man down the road bringing a ladder and pulling it out. Another rather unusual appeal to the police was made by Mrs. Andrews:

> Next door complained all the time that my TV was blaring too loud. I got fed up and phoned the police to verify that the volume wasn't unreasonable.

The police apparently turned up in response to Mrs. Andrews' call but she never revealed what the adjudication was.

There was another larger category of incidents recounted by respondents where calling the police was the obvious and necessary thing to do but where the expectations by the callers of what the police might achieve were unrealistically high. One such type of incident, not surprisingly, was the domestic dispute involving violence, seen or overheard by neighbours. The police were not at all keen to become involved in such cases for many reasons but nevertheless it was difficult to see what else the anxious neighbours could have done other than call the police. As Mrs. Jordon (quoted earlier) said:

> This woman was getting kicked to death but we were the only ones who would ring the police. The neighbours were all watching but nobody would ring the police . . . . of course two hours after you ring them they come and by that time it's all over.

When the Sands' young woman neighbour had come round one night with her children because her cohabitee had shoved her outside and locked the door they phoned the police but were apparently told that:

> the police could not intervene in a domestic dispute.

Mr. Cope told how:

> this woman was hitting her child with a strap outside on the grass. I went over and told her to leave it alone. You can imagine the kind of things she said. So I called the police but they didn't do anything. She just shut the door in their face.

The commonest situation which led to disappointment in what the police could realistically achieve was teenager fights, gangs of teenagers threatening someone, or children or teenagers causing damage to someone's property and not responding to appeals to stop or go away. Understandably people got frightened or angry in these circumstances and felt that they were helpless to do anything themselves. Threatening to call the police was the only card they held. A typical instance was the experience of Mr. Hilsden:

> There was load of black kids out the front fighting and making a terrible noise. It looked like they were going to damage my front fence. I went out and tried to send them off but I got a load of abuse.

Mr. Hilsden had already been to see the mother of the family and got threatened by her with a bread knife. So he telephoned the police:

> The sergeant said there wasn't much they could do. I said if he didn't send someone there'd be an injury. The sergeant said if there was would I be prepared to be a witness in court. I said no and slammed down the phone. They weren't bloody interested. They're chicken.

Mrs. Gatehouse had an unpleasant experience while she was working in the launderette one evening:

> The glass window was being banged and knocked. I told the kids off, they were only about ten or twelve, and I got a lot of cheek and abuse. They wouldn't go away so I phoned the cops . . . . they said they'd be along in five minutes but I'm still waiting, they're useless.

The police experience was of course that in the majority of similar cases where they had arrived on the scene, the culprits had vanished. Mrs. Donaldson telephoned because of fighting and disturbance outside but:

they took so long getting here they'd gone by the time they came.

Mrs. Rawlings gave another example, one where she had not herself been involved:

> There were these boys and girls inside this garage up to no good. This policeman comes along and chases them off. Five minutes later they were back. They knew he wouldn't be back.

It was not therefore surprising that the police showed reluctance to drive to the scene of fights or vandalism knowing that for them and others it would be a futile exercise unless there were witnesses or victims who had proof positive of the identity of offenders. Mr. Aston in common with many other respondents did not understand this point:

> I only called them once, after that I never bothered again. The flats opposite were being built and I watched several youths who were chucking bricks through the large front windows. I telephoned the police, he said 'Did I know their blooming names and addresses?' I said 'No, I don't, but they're doing it _now_'. They never came, so what's the use?

Ms. Stayne complained that several people including herself had repeatedly called the police over the previous summer because:

> they should stop the big kids going on to the rec, it was awful, all swearing at you and breaking the seats for the little ones.

She said the police never came which was the same complaint as Mrs. Urquart who had been frightened and nearly hit by a firework thrown over the garden wall around the time of bonfire night. Mr. Cutler, a retired divorced man living in a block of flats, had had his car dented on two different occasions while it was parked outside the flats:

> I rang the police each time about the damage but they didn't come out to see me. They said there was nothing they could do.

Mr. Cutler was pleased that they had come to investigate a bad case of vandalism at his flats in which someone had:

> climbed an eight foot fence at the back and completely destroyed the rotary clothes drier and left it all mangled, they'd also emptied the garden shed and thrown all the tools over the garden.

This attack on the clothes drier happened to be one of a number which took place over a short period. Accounts such as this suggested that the police put a fairly low priority on cases of reported damage and nuisance which they were unlikely to be able to do much about but that if a number of similar complaints kept coming in, they felt some investigation was required. This happened in the case of Mrs. Higgins, who along with other respondents resident in the same street, complained of the nuisance, noise and frequent vandalism of teenagers returning from a particular disco late on Friday nights:

> We had a lot of other neighbours complained scores of times but they (the police) came too late or they never came at all. They did something in the end though. I think they lay in waiting one night in the gardens behind the hedges and got them. It's been better since.

Nevertheless, Mrs. Higgins' verdict on the police was that:

> They don't do their job properly at all.

A similar story was told by Mr. Dale whose family had been harassed by the noise and danger to children of motorcycles using the footpath at the back of his house as a scrambling track. After a number of futile calls to the police, Mr. Dale suggested that came on a likely night before the trouble started in order to catch them at it. The police came and did in fact catch the culprits which was just as well, as apparently Mr. Dale's next plan was going to be to fix piano wire across the path at the average height of the neck of a motorcyclist.

Demands on the protective and detective powers of the police in cases of nuisance and vandalism were taken to extremes by the Riley family who almost seemed to be demanding a twenty four hour police presence. At each of three interviews with the family over eighteen months they said they had called the police on numerous occasions in recent months. The following situations were cited as the provocations: a neighbour's vicious dog, cars and motorcycles parked on the grass outside the flats, teenagers tearing round on motorcycles late at night, children throwing stones at their children, people throwing stones and bottles at the Riley's windows, a neighbour refusing to return a ball thrown into his garden by a Riley child. The Rileys complained that police either never came, or came several days later, or if they came and saw the culprits:

> they just tell them to go away and then when the

police have gone they just come straight back.

or:

> they just warned him (the owner of the vicious dog)
> but it didn't do any good, he still lets it out.

In the case of the Rileys the frequent calls to the police seemed to be a way of hitting back against the surrounding neighbours by whom they felt threatened. The Rileys were an extreme example but many of the other cases quoted above also suggested that the police were sometimes used as weapons in fighting ongoing hostilities, to prove that the caller had right and the law on their side, to show disliked others that they could not get away with behaviour of that kind.

About fifteen per cent of all respondents showed a very optimistic opinion of what extra police patrolling could be expected to achieve. Some seemed to want the estate to be literally swamped with policemen in the hope that this would eradicate all nuisance and crime and maintain total peace and security. For example Mr. Andrews said:

> There should be a lot more patrolling. Mobile foot patrols you know in pairs in the evenings and they should go round the alleys where there's been those attacks. And with the cars as well, they should have a constantly varying pattern so that they visit every part of the estate at different times each night. And they should get rid of the bookies' shop and make a proper police station on the estate.

Similarly, Mrs. Ewer was convinced that more patrols would effectively prevent vandalism:

> There's just not enough policemen. Bus shelters get broken, houses get burgled, phone boxes never work. They've just planted a whole new batch of trees, half of them won't see the summer. The kids wouldn't be destructive if there was more cops around. On bikes would be better though, you don't see much in a car.

Mrs. Mulpepper said:

> There should be a lot more on foot or on bikes so they can see where the damage is being done, they'd catch them if they patrolled often enough.

And Mrs. Rawlings said:

> More police would make the kids more wary, knowing a cop might come along at any time. There should

definitely be more of them. I'm frightened to go
out on my own at night.

Some of this category of respondents seemed almost to be
asking for a secret police state to be set up on Omega.
Miss Ballance wanted a considerable increase in police
patrolling especially at night and wanted them in plain
clothes and accompanied by Alsatian dogs. Mrs. Arthur
wanted a policeman in every street and Mr. Fleet said:

> It would benefit everyone if we saw policemen
> walking about, they don't come round nearly often
> enough on foot. And the pandas, you can see them a
> mile off, they should have all unmarked cars so
> nobody knows they're there and that would deter
> people.

Such views suggested that there was a substantial
proportion of residents who felt totally dependent on
outside support in this case the police; who seemed to feel
there were no resources within themselves or their local
neighbourhood which could cope with the problems caused by
bored or disaffected youth or by the behaviour of a minority
of antisocial or deviant individuals. Since however
residents did appear to hold the police responsible for
maintaining not only law and order but peace and quiet and
conformity too, on Omega estate, it was inevitable that they
were seen to be failing.

There were however things they could have done to improve
the police image and the temper of the householders. One
was touched on when offences against residents were analysed
earlier in the chapter that is, the lack of communication as
to what happened in the case. This complaint occurred in
relation to other kinds of police call-out too. Mr. Dobson
had witnessed a serious accident between a car and a
motorcycle outside his house and had been the first to call
the police:

> They said I would be wanted as a witness but they
> never came back to say what happened. I never
> heard.

Obviously Mr. Dobson felt involved in the incident and let
down at not being told the sequel. The natural division of
labour would surely have been for the estate beat policeman
to call round to tell persons who had reported offences or
other incidents what had happened in the case. Even if
there was nothing much to tell, the payoff in terms of
police-public relations would surely have been worth it.

In fact there was evidence at that time that liaison between the beat policeman and the officers at the subdivisional station responsible for deploying the panda cars and detectives was not very efficient. A notable example occurred during the study when there was an indecent assault on the estate one afternoon. The incident was reported immediately, the victim was questioned and made a statement, a search for the suspected man was set in motion, yet, the following morning the beat policeman was on duty unaware of the incident. Another example was given by Ms. Billing who lived directly opposite one of the schools which was vandalised each vacation. The beat policeman had tried to enlist local support in preventing this happening:

> He came round and called on all the houses here and told us to ring up if we saw anything. Well we did, several times over the summer, me and other neighbours, we saw kids in there, doing damage. And at no time did the police ever come. So we just gave up.

The importance of the human face of the police was clearly of great importance. Those respondents who had a favourable view of the police and the job they did often revealed in their comments their appreciation of the manner in which the police handled their case. Mrs. Ash recounted:

> There was all this drunken shouting at 1 a.m. in the back alley. Our back gate was smashed in. We telephoned the police and they came straight away and stopped it. Then they told us not to worry they'd come back because they'd stay in the area to see it was alright.

Mrs. Knight lived in a block of flats inhabited mainly by old people who had all been disturbed by a stranger going round the flats and asking to come in for a glass of water. She said:

> The police gave us all a little card after that with the police number on it to put by our phones.

Mr. Lonhro had answered a knock on the door one evening and been severely beaten up by his brother-in-law:

> I was in a really bad way. We called the police and two of them in a panda came very quickly. They said it wasn't their area but they were nearest when the message came. They ascertained the facts, sent for an ambulance to get me to hospital, and then went and arrested my brother-in-law. He was taken to court.

Mr. Pratt had favourable words to say about the police even though he had been stopped for drunken driving and subsequently taken to court and convicted:

> They came to see me the next morning and they were fine, very decent. It was my own fault.

The Musgroves had apparently been treated courteously when:

> someone complained about the noise when we had a party, they were alright, very pleasant (the police) and we just turned it down.

Mr. Rutter described the police reaction to an accident his wife had:

> She wrapped the car round a lamp post up the road. Two pandas came. This cop saw it had no tax but he let her off. I call that decent. She was shook up enough.

However while an efficient system of follow-up visits to households reporting incidents and more attention to human relationships would have undoubtedly increased resident satisfaction with police the major problem was the unrealistic expectations of many residents about what the police could or should do. Many peoples' first recourse was to the police when anything at all, including long festering resentments, threatened the social equilibrium. Ekblom and Heal (1982) researching in a working class area of a northern city found a very similar situation. They called the police role 'social first aid'. Their account of the psychology of calls to the police described exactly the circumstances of many of the cases already presented in this chapter and the previous one:

> Complainants seemed to want of the police some sort of authoritative acknowledgement, from a figure representing the state or society at large, that wrong had been done to them, and that they were deserving of justice and sympathy. The failure of the police to take a complaint seriously was unsatisfying because it could deny both justification and justice. In cases where callers could feel themselves unequivocally aligned with the police (and the rest of society) against a common vilified foe, a sense of justice was enhanced.

Where this did not happen the 'they don't care about us' phenomenon seen already in tenant-housing department relations, was repeated with regard to police.

But the solution to this problem was not to flood the estate with more and more police as many residents believed but to try to get the estate to take on more first aid itself. The first step towards this would have to be educating the residents to a greater understanding of their own situation and of the police role. A series of well publicised public meetings held by the police could make a start. Such meetings were successful in similar circumstances on a bad estate in Exeter (Moore and Brown, 1981). Simple charts could demonstrate that the estate was not a den of organised crime; that the city centre was more dangerous; that the high offence rate was predominantly accounted for by youths and young men committing criminal damage, petty thefts, vehicle thefts and getting involved in brawls. The police could explain the different jobs of the beat policeman, the panda patrols and the CID. They could discuss the practical limitations on catching vandals or intervening in domestic or neighbour disputes. They could open up the question of whether the heavy retribution demanded by residents would always be the best outcome for youthful misdemeanours, and whether parents, teachers and community organisations might not take more responsibility for young people's activities on the estate. Above all on a troubled estate like Omega it seemed necessary to demonstrate to residents that their peace and quiet, their property, their protection, was of concern to the police. Omega badly needed this reassurance.

In Britain there is no realistic alternative to the police as an all purpose round the clock peacekeeping community welfare service. To do this well is the most important function of the police force. Ekblom and Heal (1982) emphasised that the provision of social first aid provides for police:

> the opportunity of meeting the public in a helpful,
> as opposed to adversarial role.

For the youth on Omega it was the adversarial role which they knew most about (see Chapter 9) but a well resourced policy of community policing as advocated by Alderson (1979) and Scarman (1982) could have helped to change that experience.

7 Families

Sixty two per cent of the householders interviewed had children under the age of nineteen living in the house. Fifty five per cent of these reported at least one problem they had encountered in bringing up the children which they related directly to living on Omega.

The history of Omega as an overspill estate for industrial workers' families in the late fifties was explained in Chapter 2. Omega was designed with families and children in mind. Although one can in retrospect, and some people did at the time it was planned, criticise a development which within the first three years of building was made up of ninty five per cent three or four bedroomed accommodation and thus prescribed a population of families with young children, the council plan was a rational and urgent, if shortsighted, response to the housing crisis of the time. By 1966 they had built some flats for the elderly and for young couples but even then eighty seven per cent of the households on the estate contained a family. The average number of persons per dwelling on the estate was 4.2. There were no three generation families.

In the early years therefore there was a situation whereby a quarter of the population was under five and another quarter was of school age with the parental generation bunched between twenty and forty five. It was a most bizarre and skewed age distribution. Residents who had lived on the estate then always commented on the numbers of children. Mrs. Andrews, the mother of a sixteen year old son, remembered when the close of twelve houses she lived in contained fifty two small children. In theory there would seem to be nothing wrong with a 'children's village', a community of young parents all experiencing the same pleasures and vicissitudes, sharing tasks, organising mutual babysitting. And for some respondents it had evidently been something like that in the early days. As Mrs. Sands who lived in a row of nine terraced houses pleasantly situated by a small green said:

> We were always in and out when the children were young. We all got on well and helped each other out. We were all very home-orientated and the kids knew the insides of all the houses.

But it evidently did not work like that for everyone. Others remembered the years differently:

> It was all wrong from the start. Whole estate in a turmoil for ten years, thousands of kids. Now it's slowed down. In a few years everything'll be dead.

Certainly from the early days, one factor contributing to the bad reputation from the authorities' point of view was the high level of social services' involvement demanded by the unsettled families. Also from the start medical practitioners were constantly being asked to provide evidence of nervous breakdowns or depressions caused by living on the estate in order to support applications for a transfer to another estate. Thus social workers, medical personnel and housing staff had early cause to look upon the estate as a burden.

Omega was nearly twenty five years old at the time of the study. And although the estate had had what the housing department referred to as a 'fairly regular turnover' there was still a large number of the original population of teeming children still around in the shape of youths and girls in their teens and early twenties. In 1981 there were two and a half thousand children between ten and nineteen living on the estate, an area of 250 acres. This represented over a quarter of the total population. If the amenities and support systems were inadequate to cope in the early days of the estate then the position barely improved as the children grew up. It is against this background that the problems of bringing up children on the estate must be viewed. And it was in this context of the estate as a community __planned__ for family living that some of the findings came as a surprise.

Families with children were the least happy category living on Omega. Less than half of families with schoolage children had wanted a tenancy on Omega. On the other hand two thirds of pensioners, young couples without children, or families with grownup children said they had wanted to come to the estate. This latter group (about a fifth of households) were, on other counts too, amongst the most satisfied, settled, friendly and active residents interviewed. The difference in stated original wish to be housed on the estate could perhaps be attributable to rosy memories in retrospect since, once the children were grownup, these families' problems were largely behind them; or it could be quite simply that the estate had got even less popular as a place to bring up a family as the children of the first settlers became teenagers and added to the estate's already poor reputation. Whatever the reason it became evident that on almost all measures related to satisfaction with estate life it was the families with children of school age who came out worst (see Table 2). They were the most likely to be victimised; less than half of them said that their neighbours were friendly while well over half the pensioners and no less than eighty per cent of the families with grownup children felt surrounded by friendly neighbours. Families with children were most likely of all categories to complain of having neighbours who definitely caused them trouble or conflict; and most markedly of all, while less than a quarter of the other categories wanted to move off the estate, over forty per cent of the families with school age children wanted to move elsewhere. Was there any simple explanation for all this? When respondents who were not happy with their neighbourhood or the estate itself, were asked why not, the answer was always, whatever category of respondent, something to do with 'other people'. Some respondents also mentioned factors inherent in the design, amenities or location of the estate, but overwhelmingly the first and foremost reason was 'people'. An interesting point to emerge was that the young couples and the pensioners who as groups tended to have come to Omega of their own volition and did not want to move away, were also by far the most likely to have relatives on the woman's side also living on the estate. That factor alone probably accounted in large part for the sense of satisfaction and belonging expressed by the youngest and the oldest of the adult generation.

But the difference on nearly every count between the two

Table 2

Comparison of families with other categories of resident on Omega; percentage of each category

	Families with school age children	Families with grown up children	Young single or couples	Elderly and retired	All categories of respondent
Wanted to live on Omega	45	67	67	67	56
Want to move from Omega	42	29	22	24	34
Feel neighbours are friendly	47	81	33	52	54
Have troublesome neighbours	57	48	44	52	53
Have relatives on Omega	38	29	56	71	42
Victimised in previous 2 years	57	57	44	43	53

types of families i.e. those with school age children and those with children grownup, must be related to other factors of lifestyle since only around one third of the families of either type had relatives on the estate. From the figures therefore, we were left with three (not mutually exclusive) possible explanations: the estate was just not a convenient suitable environment for bringing up families; or the lifestyle of families within that environment inevitably provoked conflict with and disapproval from other residents which reflected back on the families' own morale; or that families had less choice than any other category of applicant as to where they accepted suitable housing. Let us explore these possibilities further.

THE ESTATE AS A FAMILY ENVIRONMENT

Since, as was emphasised before, the entire estate was planned with children in mind, it was surprising that so little provision had been made for the safe play of children. For example the official play areas consisted of two playgrounds within two grass parks, the larger of which was right in the centre of the estate and cut through by an open smelly ditch. This park was so large and, at night, so dark, that people were often afraid to cross it. Railings and low fences lined some parts of the parks but some areas were open to the road and all had to be approached by crossing thoroughfares. This meant that cautious parents accompanied their children to the play areas which incidentally provided no seats for parents. The park and play areas could be a half mile walk from some parts of the estate. During the study the local paper headlined the death of a five year old boy who had run straight from one of the play areas out onto a road. The incident, not for the first time, aroused a barrage of complaints and grievances from residents which were the subject of a newspaper article two days later. The comments reported by parents corresponded closely to those made by our respondents which will be quoted shortly:

> Few children use the play area because parents are frightened to leave their children there unsupervised. An eighteen inch wall is no barrier to a child.

> Fifteen and sixteen year olds hang around the area in the evenings but the younger ones rarely play there.

> Even when my daughter was about seven, I worried about her because the area is not enclosed. It

98

needs a high fence round it to stop children going onto the road.

The play area is too close to the car park as well as the main road. During the lunch hour the road is very busy with traffic coming home from the factory.

The park beyond the play area is even less protected, it only has a flimsy fence round it. And there has been a lot of trouble in that park with a number of men flashing and interfering with the children.

Apart from the official play areas most of the cul de sacs and closes had small greens at the end of them; the blocks of flats and maisonettes all had large empty areas of grass around them; there were patches of waste ground which were perhaps originally intended for garages or allotments; one corner had railway embankments; and very near the estate was wild land, partly waste with drains, holes and ditches in it, and partly agricultural. All of these places provided scope for the activities of children playing football, scrambling with bicycles or motorbikes or just hanging about. Apart from the greens in the closes there was nowhere safe for the younger child to play unsupervised. And even in the closes and cul de sacs there was a problem with traffic. Mrs. Disley referred to earlier years:

All the kids were little and we used to have to watch them playing so we'd all stand out and talk to each other.

She had found this a good way of making friends with the neighbours. But now her children were older Mrs. Disley complained:

The kids just don't know what to do with themselves, always hanging about. There's not much for them to do. The youth clubs are for the older ones and ours just have to play in the street. In the winter they only go out if they're with us. In the summer it's different, they can go to the park so long as they're home before dark.

Mr. and Mrs. Anthony lived just across the road from the smaller recreation ground but said they never let their six year old daughter out to play on it.

It's dangerous, not supervised, the paddling pool is always full of glass, it's unusable.

Mrs. Sands from the same area with a seven year old daughter said:

99

There's a playground right here, it used to be looked after by a caretaker who stopped dogs going in and locked it up at night. This has stopped. Dogs foul the pool, there's broken glass everywhere and teenagers use it at night.

The Tibbets were a family with three children between six and twelve but the children were allowed only to play in the close where they lived. Though they lived near to the park they were not allowed to play there:

The main problem is the teenagers on motorbikes, and they rip up the goalposts and throw them in the brook. They should cover the brook, it's terribly smelly. But there's not a lot for kids to do.

The problem was greatest for those who lived in the flats. Mr. and Mrs. Scully lived in one of the large complex of blocks of flats with their four year old son. Though they looked out onto the play area for the flats they would not let their boy play there.

There's always gangs of teenagers, twelve or thirteen year olds, hanging around with bottles.

Consequently Mrs. Scully took the child every day to the park where she stayed with him while he played about. But they were not happy with the situation. Mr. Scully said:

We're pretty down at the moment because we think we'll never be able to get a council house with a garden for Barry while he's still young enough to enjoy it. The wife gets very frustrated being locked up here all day.

The Scully's application for a house of course would not be priority since they had only one child and were adequately housed. The Rileys said that if the children played inside their flat the people below complained, but they could not play outside on the grass round the flats because of dogs, cars and parked motor cycles and no way of stopping them getting on to the road. The Ewers lived in a similar flat with their eighteen month old daughter. Mrs. Ewer said that because there were no fences round the flats:

I can't even hang out the washing without putting her in her pushchair, and getting it down the stairs and up again, or getting her looked after by someone else.

The traffic along the roads of the estate was a very real danger as the newspaper story demonstrated. Some of the

100

roads were fast through routes for cars; buses too were a hazard for playing children. Numerous respondents mentioned the same odd fact referred to here by Mrs. Riley:

> They used to have humps in the main road, but they took them up and never put them back again. They were very good at slowing down the traffic but they said they were only an experiment and took them up. The very next day there was an accident there.

The mystery of the missing road humps was never solved. Every respondent who mentioned them said how useful they had been which suggested that the experiment had been a success. Yet instead of being extended to other long through roads they were taken up and the road made an invitation to fast traffic once more; and at the expense of injuries even lives.

To summarise so far, the estate lacked safe outdoor play areas for preschool children where parents could sit together and watch. This lack was felt particularly badly by mothers living in flats with no gardens or fenced off areas. For schoolage preteen children there were the parks or recreation grounds with playgrounds in them but these had to be approached across busy main roads and were usually a fair way from home, not maintained, not enclosed, not supervised, did not have seats for parents who wanted to accompany their children, and were often taken over by teenagers. Mr. and Mrs. Rawlings summed up some of these points:

> Take the recreation ground. The kids can't use it never on a Saturday or Sunday, because it's all football teams who probably don't even live here. We're the ratepayers and we can't use the public grounds! So the kids play in the street They can't even cut across the park if they're training. Then there's all the sixteen and seventeen year olds standing smoking because they've nothing else to do, they congregate round the swings. You can hardly expect them to sit in the library reading, can you?

So it was that the middle age range of children played mostly on the patches of grass round flats, maisonettes, by the roads, and at the ends of the small roads and closes, and inevitably ended up damaging something or annoying someone. The problems were worst of all, of course, in the holiday times. Ms. Drew in her ground floor maisonette said holidays were particularly bad:

> There's so many parents out working and don't make

any arrangements for the kids so, of course, they get into trouble. They get so fed up they just do anything they can to annoy you, just for the excitement. The pub is full of under age kids drinking. There's a group round here who sniff glue and go round starting fires.

Ms. Drew had a sister living in the USA and she was quite clear what was needed:

The schools should run organised holiday schemes for the kids. In the States the schools are open for the kids and they do all kinds of activities with them. Or they can go on camps and things. It's not expensive, everybody does it. We could do with a system like that here.

There had been in fact for a few years something called an adventure playground which in the holidays was run by two community workers and volunteers, often students. It took place in the church hut and on a site on the waste ground which was gradually being improved. It offered the opportunity for painting, craftwork and games, and sometimes there were day trips out. The adventure playground was started on the initiative of a local councillor and a local community worker. It was undoubtedly a good thing, a good start, but there were the difficulties that a child must register his or her attendance, that it was closed at weekends and that it could cater for only sixty children.

There were of course a number of organised recreational and sporting activities open to children on the estate which took place in the school gymnasium, other halls and huts or the large well equipped sports hall. Clubs existed for table tennis, judo, gymnastics, football and many other activities. But a club had to be joined, a subscription paid, attendance planned, and most clubs operated just one night per week. As Mrs. Rawlings said:

You can't go and play table tennis unless you've got £10 and what kid's got that so they're not allowed in.

The community association had suggested that the sports hall could be used at least on one day a week as a sports' centre where children and young people could drop in and pay so much each time to use the facilities. But the council could not provide regular staff to open the hall. And as with the adventure playground numbers would inevitably be limited to less than a hundred regulars. It was this fact that there were thousands, not hundreds, of children confined within the estate at weekends and half terms and holidays which

102

made the scale of the problem too great to be solved by any one new scheme or amenity. Unless that is, as Ms. Drew suggested, the schools were to be kept open, provisioned with materials and supervised on a fulltime basis.

It was evident that the estate as planned and built had not been provided with the recreational amenities necessary to cope with the foreseeable, intended even, influx of families with large numbers of children. It was quite understandable that such families if given a choice would prefer one of the smaller estates. Smaller estates tended to be more popular and the more stable population meant that people had known each other longer and may have identified more closely with their neighbourhood. Mr. Cope made a salient point, often echoed by other respondents who had been brought up in one of the old slum areas of the city which had been demolished in the fifties:

> It was never like this round the backs, yet we never had nowhere to play but the street. But there was never a locked door, no need. A kid could pop into any house and get some tea. We were all very close and if you did anything wrong your Dad put you right and marched you along to apologise. No-one ever called the police.

Mr. Cope was referring to a city centre area of a few hundred households before the war. There were nearly three thousand households on Omega.

But what was chiefly a problem of nuisance, noise and minor vandalism in the case of bored and trapped children, became something more serious in the case of hordes of teenagers with their need for excitement, a social life and something to do in the evenings. For those who liked joining organised activities there was an Air Training Corps, an Army Cadet Force, the Venture Scouts and all the one night a week sports and games mentioned before. But only a minority were interested in or could afford this kind of structured pastime. Then there was the community centre youth club open week nights and the secondary school youth club open one or two evenings a week. There was a Friday night disco a mile or so into the city. Add to this minimal provision the fact that at the time of the study around twenty per cent of the teenagers who had left school were unemployed. There was no cafe to meet in during the day, nowhere but the pubs to meet in the evenings, nowhere for the West Indian teenagers to go to play their loud reggae music, nowhere even to sit and eat the take-away fish and chips. And when the boys with the motorbikes scrambled on the waste land somebody called the police. And when teenage groups gathered on the stairways of the flats playing transistors somebody opened a front door and shouted at them to go away. So they drifted into the town centre to sit in Woolworth's cafeteria, or they got into trouble. Mrs. Overton said:

> There's not a lot for them on any estates. I find it strange because I come from London and there was always something to do. I never had to go into a pub till I came here. They need something to keep the kids off the streets. I won't let Martin into town which he sulks about. But some parents seem glad to be rid of their kids, they're always hanging about. Maybe I'll be glad to get rid of mine when they're older!

THE PEER GROUP INFLUENCE ON CHILDREN'S BEHAVIOUR

Most parent respondents had worried at one time or another about their children getting into trouble. These worries are natural enough in parents anywhere and are certainly not confined to council estates, even council estates of bad repute. But everyone on Omega knew firsthand of children in their vicinity or at school with their own children who had been in trouble with authority. Almost one in five of juvenile males over ten years old was apprehended by police in any one year. But it was sheer numbers which made the impact both physically and psychologically. Two and half thousand teenagers called Omega home. Thus all estate parents were very much aware of the constant potential opportunities for wrong doing which their children inevitably encountered daily.

The worries of respondent parents tended to be expressed as fear of their children growing up 'rough' through contamination by the 'wrong company' or else they focussed on the inadequacies of the schools on the estate, particularly the secondary school. Mr. and Mrs. Liffey who had bought a house on the estate as a means of getting a foothold in the owner occupier market explained:

> I can't see anyone with a family wanting to come and live on the estate because of firstly the schools and secondly the reputation of the children here. We certainly wouldn't want to have kids in this sort of environment because our kids would be different to other kids on the estate. We'd encourage them to do homework and study and read books and so on,

104

they'd feel different.

This of course was recognisably a middle class attitude but it was nonetheless reflected in what a number of other respondents said. For example Ms. Drew was a factory worker and had a son of five. She was on the transfer list and was determined to make a nuisance of herself to the housing department until she got accommodation in another area.

> I've got to get off the estate. I don't like the kids Darryl has to play with. I'd be really frightened to let him mix when he's older.

The Rileys had come to the same conclusion and in Mr. Riley's case it could be presumed that he was talking from experience. He had been brought up on the estate in a family of nine and blamed his own criminal record onto the company he kept. The family was on the transfer list but since their children were all boys a two bedroomed flat was regarded as adequate accommodation and they had no priority need. But Mr. Riley said:

> I'm leaving when my eldest is ten, whatever, if we haven't been offered anything better. I'll squat if necessary.

Mr. and Mrs. Sumner had a son of eight and also wanted to move away.

> Paul is very bright. He's already two classes ahead but they won't let him go up till he's eleven. He's not happy, he gets bullied. He's had his toys smashed up. The teachers are very nice but the parents give no support. The other week the parents were specially invited to go along to join in the morning service and I was the only parent to go and I had to take time off work to go. Paul has no friends. He feels different. He needs friends of his own kind.

It is of interest to note that in all other ways the Sumners were happy on the estate and not at all snobbish. They had good friends among the neighbours, particularly a nearby West Indian couple whom they saw every day, and they frequented the local public house. Their son's prospects at the estate schools seemed to be their only reason for being determined to move. Mrs. Ewer with a preschool daughter said:

> I've been put off the schools on Omega by my friend's experience. The teachers don't teach the kids, they're frightened of them. There's not enough discipline. And there's no school uniform so

you can't ring them up when you see them hanging about. The kids are always off school, smoking, drinking, playing radios on the stairs, they seem to wander about all day long.

The Ewers wanted to move.

But moving was not the only solution for parents who identified the chief threat as being the undisciplined atmosphere and peer group influence of the estate schools. Mr. Ponting for example was extremely worried about schooling on the estate and wanted to move. But Mrs. Ponting was so happy there and had so many good neighbours that she had persuaded her husband to remain so long as their children were sent to 'better' schools off the estate. She had gone into the question and decided that the Roman Catholic schools in the city offered more discipline, structured teaching and smaller classes. So though not Roman Catholic themselves, they had sent their son to the Roman Catholic primary school and were pleased with the result:

He needed pushing and it separated him from his friends which was a good thing.

The Dowtys were intending to do the same thing because their eight year old son had been involved in a number of fights at his local primary school and:

he needs discipline and it will take him away from his friends.

A number of respondent parents had decided to take the step of finding an alternative school not on the estate at the secondary school stage only. Mrs. Ash said:

I used to hear them coming out and the rough language they used. I was appalled and swore that my girls would never go there.

Although all the city state schools were in theory open to all city children this depended upon acceptance by the head teacher. The choice was not realistically open to the majority of parents on Omega. The schools with the best reputations tended still to require school uniforms, and time, distance, complicated transport arrangements, and expense, all weighed against the effort. Mr. and Mrs. Overton had considered the possibility. They were having a lot of trouble with their twelve year old son who was disobedient, disruptive and aggressive, both at home and school. Mrs. Overton said:

We would have preferred Martin to go to a different school, he's a right little bugger and he needs a lot of discipline, like at the old grammar but we heard it costs a fortune just for the rugby gear and then there's the bus fares and we couldn't afford it.

The case of the Jordan's son Michael was interesting in this regard. Mr. Jordan said:

The teacher at the school really encouraged Michael and he wanted to go the old grammar. We put his name down but we got refused and he had to go here. They don't really give you a choice but they pretend they do. So he didn't get the discipline and there was no-one to push him. He was very disappointed he didn't get to the grammar, he lost heart and he just skived all the time. We couldn't stop him and he left the day he could.

About fifteen per cent of respondent families with school age children were sending a child to school off the estate.

For those parents however who had decided to remain on the estate and had settled for the local estate schools there was always in the background the worry that by getting into the wrong company their children would get into trouble because of truancy or delinquency or both. It is perhaps worth asking at this point how realistic these worries were. With regard to truancy thirty five per cent of respondent parents with school age children had had this problem at some time and had been contacted by an educational welfare officer for this reason. The truants were, as many respondents testified, very visible on the estate but then as Mrs. Newson said:

The school is right in the middle of the estate, it's very much in the public eye.

Truancy was impossible to measure. The only objective measure of the comprehensive school's success as an educational environment which could be obtained, was the results in public examinations for CSE and GCE. Unfortunately it had to be said that these results were appalling in comparison with all the other city secondary schools. During the study eighty six per cent of school leavers had no passes in any subject. The figure was nearer fifty per cent for the city schools as a whole and better still for the Roman Catholic schools. There was justification therefore for worry by those Omega parents who did want a good academic education for their children.

On the other hand with strong motivation and encouraging parents it was possible to do well despite the prevailing non-academic environment. The Redders, the Sowters, the Clappers and the Lawsons all had children who had successfully passed some 'O' levels and a few were preparing for 'A's. As Mrs. Newson said:

It's alright if you want to learn.

Similarly Mrs. Ewer said:

It's a good school if they want to learn but if they don't there's nothing done to encourage them.

The headmaster took what he regarded as a realistic view and said that he felt the top priority for the school was to provide pastoral care and work experience. He had no illusions about the calibre of the majority of his pupils. He claimed (and as we have seen from respondent accounts he was doubtless correct) that there was a creaming off of children with parents with middle class aspirations, and of those whom the primary schools, the heads of which were still living in the grammar school era, regarded as bright, and whom they pushed to get a place at a more academic city comprehensive. He administered IQ tests from time to time out of interest and recorded an average IQ of ninety with only a handful of pupils over hundred which is the national average. Whether one believes that IQ tests measure inherited intelligence or demonstrate only an achievement or performance level determined by environmental factors and motivation, there was a rational basis for the headmaster's decisions on priority objectives.

Until the reorganisation of schools in the early seventies into local comprehensives replacing the previous secondary and grammar schools, the estate school had been a secondary modern. The brightest children passed the eleven plus and were sent to the city centre grammar schools. Whatever the drawbacks and injustices of that system, at least the place of the school within it made sense, and there was no reason to believe that the children of Omega were significantly more at an educational disadvantage than in other city areas. But to make the estate secondary into a comprehensive was clearly a mistake. It was the only school in the city in that category to have an almost totally working class catchment area. It was still a secondary modern in all but name but the few bright and motivated children were hopelessly outnumbered compelled to struggle against the prevailing non-academic ethos. Therefore just where the need was greatest for a child to have an emotionally stable home, parents supportive of the school and parents interested in school progress and monitoring homework, these factors were least available. In a school taking in a wider social mix and where to be academically proficient was not to be different, a child might still have made progress without parental support, but in Omega you had to be very tough and determined and confident to succeed. No-one could pretend equality of educational opportunity for the children of Omega. The fundamental fault lay in the creation in the first place of a one class housing estate of such size with such a foreseeable skewed age distribution, and with the deliberate intention of its being selfcontained and serviced by its own amenities, in other words, isolated.

And of course the same planning fault contributed to the probability of, and impact of, delinquency on the estate. A lot of respondents were very much alive to this. Mrs. Pearson said:

> It's a very large council estate and it's just the right age for getting into trouble. All the kids born here are fifteen to twenty years old, ripe for trouble. Teenagers anywhere get into trouble but there's too many here.

Or Mrs. Newson:

> There's so many teenagers here, much more than other parts of the city, and nothing at all to do. They're so bored it's no wonder they get into trouble. They can't be blamed.

Some respondents gave some feature of the estate itself as a cause of delinquency but the largest category blamed boredom, lack of discipline and lack of supervision by parents. As Ms. Redder put it:

> Parents should stay in and look after their kids then there wouldn't be any problem with teenagers. Mother's place is in the home. I had to fight with my old man to stay at home, he wanted me to get a job, but I'm very old fashioned. Too many kids have to make their own meals all the time. When both parents are at work that's when you get the problems. They don't see the kids so they don't know what they're up to.

The Copes expressed the same attitude.

> A lot of parents don't seem to care where their children are. Ours always had to be in at a reasonable hour and we never went out for years so we could be at home with them in the evenings.

Ms. Worthy said:

> A lot of parents don't bother, so long as the kids
> are out of their way they don't care. That's when
> all the trouble starts. Roger doesn't often go out
> but when he does I always want to know where so that
> if I want him I can fetch him if need be. Some
> parents don't care about their children out late at
> night. In the summer even toddlers are out all
> hours hanging round the pubs.

There were numerous examples of this point of view.
Mrs. Lucas expressed it plainly.

> It's up to each parent, you can't blame the estate.
> My kids were never out on the estate at night so
> they never got into trouble. I always knew where
> they were.

WAYS OF ADAPTING

It is relevant here to mention the work of Harriet Wilson
(1980, 1982) on parental behaviour and delinquency. Unlike
the current study, Wilson's research aimed to produce
statistical data which could be used in an analysis of
causal relationships. In both of her major studies she
investigated samples of socially handicapped families
(defined as having five or more children, known to social
services, unskilled manual workers) living in deprived inner
city areas or on difficult housing estates. Within this
already very disadvantaged group she nevertheless found
clear differences in childrearing methods. Some parents
exercised very strict supervision and control over their
children's behaviour and whereabouts. Others let their
children roam freely and did not worry when they did not
know where they were or when they did not come back at
certain times. The greater the degree of social handicap
the greater the probability that the parents would be in the
'lax' category. But the strongest and most significant
correlation was that between amount of parental supervision
and the probability of delinquent behaviour by the children:

> The delinquency rate in lax families was almost
> seven times higher than that in strict families, all
> being resident in high crime areas (1982).

This is not all that surprising although as Wilson states it
is a factor which has been largely neglected by research.
It is of interest that the present study found the same
differences between 'strict' and 'lax' parents. Wilson's

hypothesis was that both the strict and the lax methods of childrearing were adaptations to the perceived environment. In the case of the strict parents:

> The environment was generally seen as a 'bad' one in which to bring up children, it was not pleasant, not safe, there were unruly children, rough or criminal elements, inadequate amenities (1980).

In addition however these parents, according to the hypothesis:

> have a degree of self confidence and status consciousness.

The lax parents may equally see the environment as bad and contaminating but feel helpless in the face of this and their other problems and therefore they hope for the best and if their children get into trouble they blame it on the very same factors of other people's children, lack of amenities, etc.

Among the thirty six families with teenage children in the households interviewed in the research there were many typical examples of Wilson's categories of both 'lax' and 'strict'. The Appendix contains descriptions of eight estate families. The lax families were characterised by a general lack of rules for the children, arbitrary discipline, a tendency to use corporal punishment, and the children mostly out of the house with their parents not knowing where they were or whom they were with. Some of the strict families were quite amazingly strict in the imposition of rules and maintenance of supervision of their children. In all the cases described the researchers collected material from parents and then independently from the teenagers to make sure that the practice fitted the theory. Of course it must not be forgotten that there is a long tradition of strict childrearing methods amongst those who regard themselves as the respectable working class and they have always differentiated themselves in this way from the roughs and, over recent generations, from the increasingly permissive middle class parents. The strict supervising parents would have been evident, indeed predominating, in any working class area and would not only be found in the deprived neighbourhoods studied by Wilson or on problem estates such as Omega. However in the example provided by Wilson (1980) and in cases presented in the Appendix some of the parents were clearly responding to specific dangers perceived as coming directly from the immediate environment. Although it may seem as if some of these parents were over-reacting, there was evidence from

111

Wilson's (1982) finding that, intuitively, they had reason
to be worried. When she separated out the figures for one
housing estate which had a significantly higher proportion
of socially handicapped families than the other six estates
from which her sample families were drawn, Wilson found that
there was a higher rate of delinquents among the strict
families (although it was still lower than among the lax
families) than was the case in the other estates. Wilson
drew the following conclusion:

> The aggregation of lax families results in a
> 'multiplier effect'; an increase in the proportion
> of such families will produce a more than
> proportional increase in vandalism and delinquency
> affecting children from supervising families who
> would otherwise be non-delinquent.

The 'multiplier effect' could be due to proportion, as
Wilson says, or, it could be suggested, it could operate by
sheer numbers, but either way the hypothesis was relevant to
the situation on Omega. Mrs. Mulpepper put the theory of
the 'multiplier factor' into plain words when she said:

> When I was a child I had three or four main friends
> round about, but round here in the summer there's
> forty or fifty children playing on that little green
> so if there's them that's easily led there's plenty
> of bad ones to lead them. There's a lot that's
> hardened, they sit on the wall and talk about coming
> out of DC like it's old hat, and they're proud of
> themselves. Lots of respectable parents can't
> understand how their kids got into trouble, good
> people whose children have got into the wrong
> company.

Only two of the teenagers in the sample of households
could be said to have been in any serious kind of trouble
(burglaries in one case, throwing bricks at passing trains
in another) but seven had been in court or officially
cautioned and sixteen others had been stopped and questioned
by police and given on the spot warnings about minor
infringements like bicycles without lights, or searched in
the course of police enquiries for no apparent reason other
than that they had been standing around. The possibility of
basically non-delinquent teenagers getting into some kind of
trouble for no greater reason than being around, or being
bored or being with a tougher mate, were illustrated in some
of the accounts in the Appendix and in Chapter 9.

There were therefore answers to the question posed at the
beginning of this chapter as to why it was, given that the

estate was planned for families with children, that families as a category were the least satisfied with life on the estate, had the most problems and that so many wanted to move away.

The answers were certainly to do with the original planning of the estate, both its physical layout and amenities, and its allocated population. If there had been a safe, enclosed, well maintained play area with seats for parents in each small area of the estate, and if there had been provision of more nursery and playgroup places, and if flats and maisonettes had been insulated and sound proofed, and had walls around them, then Omega could have been a pleasant place for families with young children. At school age and into the teens, the lack of localised play areas, the lack of drop in meeting places, sports or recreation centres, cafes or clubs, and the lack of organised provision for holiday activities, intensified the problems caused by the unnatural age distribution and the one class nature of the population. The schools in particular suffered from the lack of a social mix and the substantial proportion of disadvantaged children, factors which made it difficult for them to provide an educationally stimulating environment. Parents who had aspirations for their children found this very worrying. Parents who regarded themselves as respectable working class and who themselves did not mix with, and did not wish their children to mix with, those families they regarded as rough, tended to attempt very strict supervision of the activities of their children. The findings of Harriet Wilson suggested that these respectable supervising parents had an uphill struggle in an area like Omega where there was a substantial proportion of unsupervised children. The quotations from parents, in this chapter and in the Appendix, showed that all of these factors were appreciated by respondent parents. It was no wonder that the estate was unpopular as a place to bring up children.

8 Teenagers

Talking to the teenagers produced a picture of life on Omega very different from the stressed portrayal of the adult householders. There were three sources of teenage material: interviews with teenagers in the sample households in which there were sixty four teenagers from thirty six families, forty five of whom were successfully followed up; secondly twenty five teenagers currently in the fifth forms at the secondary school answered a questionnaire and were interviewed; thirdly one of the researchers spent many evenings and weekends with groups of teenagers who used the community centre youth club, the school youth club, and two other youth clubs off the estate which attracted Omega youth.

Omega teenagers had their roots on the estate to a degree not ever expressed by their parents. Ninty per cent of the total sample had been born on Omega or else had been so small when the family arrived there that they remembered nothing of anywhere else. Three quarters had older siblings and the majority of the teenage respondents seemed to be the youngest or next to youngest child of parents who had typically come to settle on the estate about twenty years earlier with one or two babies. Whereas a third of adults interviewed would have liked to get away from the estate altogether, only one in five of the teenage youths had a negative attitude to Omega. Girls' opinions were closer to the parental generation. While for parents it was neighbours and relatives who were significant, in the case of teenagers it was their agemates. They almost without exception claimed to have 'hundreds', or 'thousands' or even 'millions' of friends, and three quarters of those who said they liked living on the estate gave as their one and only reason that all their friends lived there. Even those who said they did not like the estate often qualified their statements as did Paul:

> Nothing to do, nowhere to go, but I like it sumtime because my freind all lives here and I no it all my life. †

One fact thus, stood out clearly that the teenagers themselves did <u>not</u> think there were too many teenagers around. Not a single teenager ever made a remark to indicate that the preponderance of teenagers on the estate was a problem in itself, or a reason for the estate being an unpopular or disliked place. Some teenagers commented on the friendliness of the estate in general:

> I like it because it's a close community and people help each other.

Gary's analysis would be difficult to support objectively but it was encouraging that he felt that to be the case. Similarly Lynn gave her subjective impression:

> Yes, I have a lot of friends and it is a small estate and everyone nos each other.

Small and friendly to the teenagers born there perhaps; large and unfriendly to many adults. The views of the minority who said they did not like living on Omega followed a very predictable pattern. 'It's a dump' said a number of teenagers who did not living on the estate. Others who disliked it said 'It's boring' though a few elaborated a little for example:

> It's too boring and there isn't no good things going on like fairs no more good discos because they only have them on special acassions.

> Aright in the summer when you go in the park and muck about or bike but nowere to go when its dark exept pubs.

---

† Misspelling in the text indicates that the quotation was taken unchanged from one of the written questionnaires administered in the school.

Or:

> There's not a lot of things to do like there is at london or something like that there should be better things to do like ice skating or fairs. one comes but only once a year.

'Boring' was a subjective value judgment and others held the view that there was in fact plenty to do on the estate. Darren wrote:

> I don't mind it because there are discos and youth clubs which you can go to if you want and recreation grounds and football fields.

Joy wrote:

> I quite like it here because it is alright when there are no fights and it has more recreation than most estates.

In marked contrast to adult respondents only three teenagers out of the total number whose views were ascertained mentioned the factor of reputation when asked if they liked living on the estate (although those who simply said 'It's a dump' might have been influenced by outsider attitudes). Patsy wrote:

> I like Omega because Ive got used to it, but other people that live out of it dislike it. Because theres been three rapings and one murder.

Peter said:

> Omega is not as bad as it seems. It has been branded by police, and anyone out of line in Omega is plastered all over the paper. It's a normal estate although it is a bit boring. But I have many good friends on the estate.

Another boy Rick said:

> It isn't really that bad and most of the people here are very nice. It is very hard when everybody gives you a tag calling you an Omega yobbo.

Three youths claimed as their reason for liking the estate those very factors which put off most people, again a minority view but worth quoting:

> I like it Because its Rough and its good to be here.

> It's great Its quite rough, lots of skinheads, teds, mods, headbangers, etc.

> Yes, Because it is the biggest and hardest place out.

As with the parental generation it became apparent that there were different categories of teenager (of course this oversimplified the situation but other measures varied with the categorisation giving it some validity). Just over half the boys and just under half the girls said they were out of the house four or more evenings a week (not counting any evening spent in a job). A third of boys and a quarter of the girls said they were out every night. Those who spent the majority of evenings at home were labelled 'homecentred'. Their activities consisted of watching television. Homecentred girls often had their boyfriends with them nearly every evening. The ones who went out most evenings were labelled 'outgoing' or 'streetcentred'. For boys, the pattern of their evenings seemed to be that they met up with the same friends every night, about eight or ten of them living in their immediate vicinity, in the streets around their homes and that they spent their time 'doing nothing much', 'mucking about', 'riding bikes', 'playing football', 'talking', 'walking about', 'playing space invaders', 'chatting up birds'; some of them 'went round my mate's' or 'went round my girlfriend's', while a very few mentioned specific activities like sports training, scrambling, working on motorcycles, and CB transmitting; some of the fifteen and sixteen year olds and a lot of the older teenagers said they went to the pub and played darts or snooker. The 'outgoing' girls also tended to meet up with others around their street but the groups seemed to be smaller, on average two to six girls, and the pattern of the evenings was to end up at somebody's house; discos, pubs and visits to town were special features punctuating the weekly routine of the girls. Only five per cent of boys and one per cent of girls in the household and school samples had ever frequented the community centre youth club however even though it was open every weekday evening. The one place therefore that was open most of the time attracted only a tiny proportion of even the streetcentred youth, who apparently preferred to spend their evenings hanging round the streets or visiting friends' houses.

It is worth pursuing the example of the youth club further since it posited a dilemma for any analysis of the estate provisions for youth. Here was what appeared to be an admirable amenity. It was run by two tough middleaged working class men who had a good relationship with the youngsters. It sold soft drinks and coffee and heavy metal music boomed out from a record player. There was also a darts room, a table tennis room, a TV lounge, a games room for pool, bar billiards and chess, a gym for badminton, indoor football and boxing, and another small room for meetings. There was a weekly disco. It organised competitions with other clubs and opportunities to go on courses and outings; and it tried to get its members involved in decorating and repair and maintenance jobs on the club premises. The club had a regular membership consisting of two core groups, one of between ten and fifteen racially mixed younger teenagers, and the other a group of about ten sixteen to eighteen year old white youths. Girls were present in a small minority. This clientele contrary to what one might expect of such a respectable sounding youth club contained some of the toughest young persons on the estate, many from large wellknown families who had older brothers with established reputations for criminal behaviour. The youth club facilities could have catered for a larger membership, and the club itself could have profited from more young people prepared to commit themselves to joining teams and taking advantage of the out of club activities offered.

From the respondents in the household samples both adult and teenager the nature of the regular youth club clientele was the reason given for them not allowing their children to go, or them not wanting to go. Audrey said:

> It's too rough, there's always fights, I wouldn't go there.

Another widely held view was that the club was a preserve of the black population which was actually completely wrong. Nonetheless Pauline said:

> I don't go there. It's packed with coloureds.

One mother said:

> I discourage him from going there because of the blacks, though I'm not colour prejudiced. It's just when you get a lot together they get excitable and it's not safe.

And a father said:

> The community centre club is plagued with blacks. They're always in groups and you can sense they're hostile to you.

Thus the club had this image of 'being rough', 'always having fights', 'plagued with blacks', none of which was true or based on the direct experience of the respondents. One or two teenage respondents had actually tried out the youth club and not enjoyed it. Michelle said:

> Everybody just stands about, they don't show films

or have games.

Games of course were exactly what were on offer if you had a partner and got there before the places were booked. Tony said:

> Me and all my mates used to go, but we don't anymore, it's only young kids now.

The explanation for these negative views was probably that some youngsters who did try out the club felt out of things, because the regulars all knew each other, and were not their usual friends and schoolmates. The much greater attendance at the school club night supported this hypothesis, even though there was in fact less to do there than in the community centre youth club with its custom built premises.

Further, when one researcher began to frequent the youth club and got to know the regulars it was evident that the majority came from the streets in the vicinity of the club. It seemed likely therefore that the youth club had become the territorial base for the streetcentred youth in the immediate area. After considerable observation of the pattern of activities of the streetcentred teenagers all over the estate the researcher concluded:

> There can not be said to be a set of common peer groups on the estate. Rather, there are many smaller cliques of same-age males ten to twenty in number perhaps engaging in streetcentred activities in their own part of the estate, though the boundaries are not defined.

The logical deduction from this conclusion was that the idea of one central club for two and a half thousand teenagers on a 250 acre estate was not only an underprovision but based on a misunderstanding of social behaviour patterns. A number of smaller clubhouses scattered over the different corners of the estate and supervised by local adults would no doubt have been wellused, each by its local streetcentred boys and girls.

Another unanticipated need was for a separate youth club for the black youth who in fact had solved the problem by taking over the youth club in an area of the city bordering on Omega. The separate clubs were not needed because of black-white hostility on the estate for as of the time of the study there was no racial problem. The races mixed at school, in sports, in the community centre and public houses as neighbours, workmates, girlfriends and boyfriends. It was simply that in their teens a section of the black youth began to identify with the Rastafarian dress and lifestyle, one integral part of which was reggae music. They wanted to listen to it, dance to it, and often got involved in assembling sound systems which would go around clubs and attract a following. The pop music records played at the Omega youth club were controlled by the youth workers and the black youth gradually dropped out and went elsewhere. These divergent paths seemed to happen naturally as an adolescent process of finding identity. Tim, a black teenager who had his own sound system explained the difference:

> When they're young they both use the clubs. But as they get a bit older, the white kid starts to save money for the deposit on a motorbike. This takes him out of the club. Of course a bit later, the motorbike thing wears off and he's back, this time into the pub, talking about football and sex. The black kid has no interest in motorbikes. They're into sound systems. And they take better care of their bodies.

Apart from the youth clubs the only other places on the estate frequented by teenagers were the two public houses. These were more popular with boys and increasingly so with the older teenagers. There were sometimes discos held at schools or community centres and clubs in neighbouring areas which attracted mainly girls. Girls were less likely to go to any local events as they grew older since they preferred to go into town nightspots with their boyfriends.

The world of the teenagers, particularly the outgoing ones, was a world psychologically if not physically apart. They seemed indifferent to, almost unaware of, parents neighbours, any adults, until they impinged on their world by complaining or intervening. This happened frequently of course but it was plain from their accounts and comments that adults were not significant as people to the teenagers. They were more like a part of the environment which occasionally you tripped over.

For example in the case of the outgoing type of white youth, unless they were heavily involved in sports training, they had to make their own entertainment of an evening, at the weekends and in the holidays. One perfectly natural activity, playing football, inevitably led to nuisance for the neighbours. Footballs bounced on parked cars, hit windows, or had to be continually retrieved from people's gardens. The grass on the greens and closes and pavements got worn down and churned up. The only way of avoiding all this was to organise a team and set off for the few legitimate pitches in the park or railway recreation ground which might be some distance away. The pitch might be occupied or there might not be time to go all that way and have a proper game or the younger teenagers might be instructed to stay in the vicinity and in any case things just did not happen that way. Richie's experience was salutory:

> We used to go over the school on the pitches there 'cos all the other pitches were being used by the men and the teams. When we did that though someone would always call the police and they told us we had to move off the school property. One time we refused to go and said there was no where else to play football. They booked us all, took down all our names, said we were going to be in trouble, but nothing ever happened.

If they stayed in the road it was worse. Roger recounted how:

> This neighbour down the road has a right good go at us if our football hits his house. He goes and phones the police but it's a laugh because no police have ever turned up.

Derek had a similar source of fun:

> There's this woman at the end. The ball's always going in her garden. We have to jump over the wall and get it ever so quickly or she rushes out and gets hold of it and won't let us have it back.

Some youths said that once neighbours had identified them as a source of trouble over something like football, they got blamed for whatever else happened in the street. Richie recounted how:

> We had this bloke, Noel, who didn't like us at all and someone smashed his lights in and on another occasion they put sugar in his petrol tank and he came over and accused us of doing it.

Similarly the Rowland boys used to go to play ball in the area round a block of flats on their road. There had then been an outbreak of graffiti over the walls of these flats and some fires started outside front doors which neighbours had reported to the police. The police had patrolled the vicinity and picked out the Rowland boys for questioning. The boys said they knew nothing about the vandalism but from that moment, Mr. Rowland had forbidden his children to go

121

anywhere near the flats so that he and everyone else could be certain that they were not responsible for any further incidents.

The other normal activity for white youths was motorbikes. There was one legitimate way to indulge in motorbike racing and that was to own your own bike and join the Speedway Club in the city. But most boys who got interested in motorbikes at thirteen or fourteen years old had to make do with borrowed rides on older boys' bikes 'on the dumps' or round the streets. Older boys had their own bikes but nowhere to go on them, nowhere to race for free. Even on the waste ground people complained of the noise and phoned the police. And of course roaring round the streets provoked numerous complaints and reports to police on the grounds of danger and the noise. To some extent the precipitation of neighbours' angry reactions added to the excitement and interest of the activities. Even the harmless and necessary undertaking of maintenance and tuning the engine got Desmond into trouble. The next door neighbour worked shifts and got understandably angry when the motorbike was started and revved while he was trying to sleep. In the interests of keeping the peace Desmond's parents insisted the bike must not be started up during the afternoons.

Thus unless parents were of the kind who did not care about what neighbours thought of them and their family there was pressure on them to restrict teenagers' footballing and biking activities. In the later teens when youths were more likely to drift into the public houses or go into the town centre these problems lessened. It was just therefore at the ages from thirteen to about sixteen when there were few places to go and nothing much exciting to do that two entirely natural and energetic outlets produced adult disapproval which gave the activities delinquent connotations which they did not deserve.

Even if teenagers stayed in or congregated in a friend's house the loud playing of pop music sparked off neighbour complaints which led to a clampdown by parents. A quarter of the teenager sample said they were subject to restrictions inside the house which usually referred to numbers of friends allowed in and noise output. While these rules were no doubt imposed mainly for the parents' own peace and quiet there were indications that the impact on neighbours was also a factor. Tony said:

> They like me to turn the records down because of the neighbours.

And it was a fact that Mr. and Mrs. Sowter drew a great deal of satisfaction from the good relationships of mutual help and consideration they enjoyed in their terrace of six houses. Mark had received a stereo system for Christmas and was explicit in his resentment of the trouble it caused:

> I can't turn it up full blast because the neighbours complain. It's pointless having a powerful system and living in a council house.

His friend Gerald agreed and said that his mother and their neighbours had not been on speaking terms for months as a result of the noise made by the playing of the boys' music centre.

It was evident that if everything teenagers did provoked disapproval they would develop a tendency not to care at all; and if teenagers were stopped from doing some things then they would do other things instead which might be less desirable or constructive. Yet the neighbours were only insisting on their right to peace and quiet in their own homes. Lower density housing, front gardens, thicker internal walls and insulation would have helped the problem of noise as was pointed out in Chapter 5. The planning which led to the disproportionate numbers of teenagers on the estate all at once, coupled with a design lay out containing no localised recreation grounds was the main factor at fault. Each area of a few hundred houses on the estate needed a recreation area and a community hut. The provision of a motorbike scrambling course on part of the waste ground bordering the estate would hardly have cost a lot. Two or three late opening coffee and coke bars complete with juke boxes and space invaders would surely have paid for themselves or, if not, would have been worth subsidising by the council. The situation was ridiculous as it was when teenagers indulging in normal non-delinquent activities such as playing football, riding motorbikes and enjoying loud pop music were discouraged from these pursuits simply because, as a consequence of the poor planning of the estate, they disturbed the peace and quiet of adults. One unusually eloquent motor bike mad fifteen year old Dan who had lived all his life on the estate but whose parents took him back to Ireland every summer wrote poignantly:

> I belong to Kerry in ireland no such thing as concrete jungles like this dump I have spent part of life living on farm surrounded by villages mountains seaside Riding my bike without the risk of being nicked its butiful in county kerry not like a dump called Omega.

9 Delinquents

Omega estate had the highest rate in the city of juveniles in trouble with police (see Table 1). One in five males aged from ten to sixteen years were apprehended each year on Omega compared with one in six on Chalkbury and the city average of about one in eight. Prosecutions were proportionally slightly more probable for those from Omega. The rate of criminal convictions of men over seventeen years was also very high, much higher at seven per cent than Chalkbury or the city average of four per cent.

It was not the purpose of this account to engage in theoretical speculation on the causes of delinquency. Many others have set themselves that task. The question was why Omega should have had <u>more</u> juvenile offenders proportionate to the population of teenagers than an estate like Chalkbury or the rest of the city. The preconditions for a high delinquency rate were certainly present in that the indices of social disadvantage found by West (1982) and Wilson (1980) to be predictive factors in delinquency were rather higher on Omega than on Chalkbury and much higher than for the city as a whole. These indices were the proportion of low income families and the proportion of families with four or more children. Omega had a higher proportion of unskilled workers, a higher unemployment rate, and twenty five per cent of Omega households contained five or more persons compared with eleven per cent in Chalkbury.

Wilson's (1980, 1982) evidence suggested that the mediating factor between social disadvantage as defined above and a high rate of apparently delinquent children was the lax parenting and lack of supervision often provided by such families; and that the larger the proportion of such families in a neighbourhood the greater the likelihood that children of socially and economically better off families would be drawn into delinquent associations. The observed fact, confirmed by the statements of Omega teenagers themselves, that half of them were out of the house most nights a week with nothing particular to do fitted the picture, as did the family case histories in the Appendix.

There remained however the question of why being out of the house and unsupervised and having nothing to do should so frequently lead to delinquency even on Omega. Since the study obtained a good deal of material on the activities of Omega teenagers it seemed worthwhile setting the facts against two recurrent (worn, familiar but still around) explanations of how such youngsters got into trouble. Either there was a subculture of deviance (Mays 1963), or since Omega was labelled delinquent, selective attention by police to estate youth led to a reactive confirmation of delinquent behaviour (Becker 1963).

SEARCHING FOR A SUBCULTURE OF DELINQUENCY

Every night about half the teenagers of Omega drifted outside their homes and congregated in loosely connected groups on the streets, closes, greens and patches of waste land. The remaining half were inside watching television, perhaps with a friend, or working at an evening job. These streetcentred groups focussed their activities on their own neighbourhood, but there were no observations or accounts of any rivalry or territorial boundaries. The central part of the estate however was somewhat different since it contained the youth club open week nights, the community centre, the public house, the chip shop and the Chinese take-away, the bookmakers and the entrance to the secondary school, as well as being the confluence of some of the main thoroughfares. Most 'happenings' happened in this area. As was the case in other locations there were groups of teenage youths and a few girls who 'belonged' in this area and could generally be found somewhere in the vicinity most evenings. They were however somehow different from the other streetcentred groups of the estate. Partly this could be accounted for by the nature of their activities since they, unlike the others, had specific places to visit in any one evening, starting at the youth club, perhaps going on to the pub, and then to the chip shop. But it also seemed to be the case that they were a rougher, tougher lot as was mentioned in the previous chapter. They were divided into an older and a younger group with about eight to ten regular males in each group, three or four girls, and fringe members who appeared now and then. The older group was all white and the younger group was mixed race. At least six of the 'central regulars' were younger members of large notorious families often of Scottish origin, with older brothers who had made names for themselves by fighting and getting into trouble. For example Jimmy, one of a family of eleven boys and one girl, said his older brothers had obtained such a reputation for fighting, that there was allegedly not a public house in the city which would allow them in. Of the regular group of older teenage males five definitely had court convictions and at least two of them had long records. Of the younger regulars two already had several court convictions. There may have been others in both groups who had a record but the subject did not arise in conversations. It was evident that here among this score of youths and the girls who associated with them was the distillation of the image of Omega youth, as it was believed to be, not only by outsiders and the press, but also by a good number of residents as well. There they were, audible and visible in the centre of the estate, sometimes provoking trouble, and sometimes getting 'nicked'. They constituted only one per cent of the teenage population and yet there was a sense in which the estate belonged to them more than anyone else because they identified themselves with the estate. The estate was their living space, their territory, and more real to them as such than it seemed to be for any other category of resident. If there was a subculture of delinquency it would have been found here.

They did seem to have the beginning of a culture because they enjoyed recalling and recounting and embellishing past exploits and events. They felt the character of the estate at any one time depended on those youths who had left school but were not yet married and that the generation previous to them had been really tough. Ally said that when he was a few years younger he could remember them coming back from a fight against the combined forces of the other estates from which they had emerged victors. These lads had now grown up and married said Ally, accounting for the fact that things were quiet at the moment. In fact the impression given was that things were now on the decline since the present fifthformers who were the up and coming generation were 'a load of pouffs'.

Their own stories were already becoming part of the oral folklore. Sandy remembered the battle between Omega School and another city school not far away.

> They came over here one night and caused trouble, fighting and that. So we went over to them the next night and there was a big fight and all the windows got smashed.

The boys regarded Omega as top estate but acknowledged that one or two others had to be watched. Other stories involved the part played by some of the boys in fighting football supporters from visiting teams and in this role they identified with the city rather than Omega. It seemed that the football fights were anticipated, even calculated. For example Nicky, one of the younger group of regulars, told how he nearly got arrested after the last big match:

> There were about a dozen of us and the same of them. We got them charging into this dead end road, then we pelted them with bricks from the top of the hill. They were breaking down trees to get sticks, and started coming up at us. They were getting all hit with bricks but they still kept coming. Then the police came so we all ran and I lost my mates.

Ally said that he did not think he would be going much this year since he had a job and if he got done they would give him a heavy fine of about £300 and it was not worth it.

During the summer of rioting in 1981 there were frequent rumours that something was going to start on Omega. One Saturday there was a build-up of numbers and of tension in the city centre, which resulted in a smashed shop window and a number of arrests. In the public house on Omega the older regulars were assembled. Ally suddenly came across with the news that someone's CB had picked up that a crowd of skinheads had wrecked the centre of town and were biking down for a fight on Omega. There was much excitement and the boys' main concern seemed to be whether they were properly dressed for a fight. Derek and Ally actually left the pub to go home and change from sneakers into Dr. Marten's boots. In fact the evening passed without incident, the phantom bikers never arrived and everyone got drunk.

The above accounts were intended to illustrate the sense in which the relationship of the central regulars to the estate was one of territoriality. They identified themselves with the estate and put themselves forward in the front line for its defence. That point made, it would be wrong to assume that these boys sought fights for trouble's sake, or that there was any subcultural value put on fighting anything but what they saw as a legitimate target. In fact they sometimes left the public house if a known troublemaker came in, saying they did not want to risk getting drawn into a fight.

They showed awareness of the rights and sensitivities of other groups in the interests of maintaining order. Near the beginning of the research for example Ally initiating the researcher into certain codes of conduct necessary if he was to go into the public house as one of the regulars, said that he would notice that the public bar was where the blacks gathered and that on one side of the bar, in the corner next to the lounge, was where the Scots always sat. You did not intrude on these territories and above all said Ally, you did not tell Scottish jokes or black jokes in there unless you were looking for trouble. On the other hand one night at a party seven American marines arrived and in the early hours a fight broke out between Bob and one of the Americans who allegedly had a knife. Immediately the regulars came to Bob's support fetching bricks for ammunition and Sandy went to get his gun. The police were called and came quickly. The boys were relieved because as Sandy admitted afterwards there was no way the regulars could have beaten those servicemen 'trained in combat'. But they had to put up the fight. Luckily no-one was arrested.

Thus fighting against something or someone seen as threatening the reputation of the estate or of those who identified with it was approved and necessary; it was the honourable way to sort something out. And fighting for something, such as one's own status, was also admired. Ally said that if you wanted to succeed on the estate, you had to be really 'hard'. Paddy was hard, he said, Mac was hard and Stewart was hard. Ally put that down to the fact that Stewart had always been beaten by his Dad which had resulted in his toughness. Ally's own father had also given him 'a rough time'. But instead of making him tough he said it had scared him. He admired his father however:

> There was this quarrel and my dad went next door to
> sort them out. My mother sent me to the phone box
> to call the police but by the time I got back he'd
> laid these four blokes out in the back garden. It
> was all over by the time the police came.

However Ally said he himself was not hard:

I got by at school by smiling a lot, and playing the fool. It works if you've got friends. Paddy was tough though he's so small and he used to stand up for me or any of his mates who got threatened.

There were therefore means other than fighting of asserting oneself in the hard value system of the central regulars which served equally if not better to maintain personal status, affirm friendly solidarity and demean chosen targets. Sandy for example had made his name in a long series of confrontations with the deputy headmaster for practical jokes and property damage resulting in seven suspensions. Another common method was verbal sparring in the form of ridicule, repartee or 'having you on'. Most of the central regulars, indeed most of the streetcentred youth in general, were barely literate as the written questionnaires given to those at school testified. But the quickwitted verbal exchanges, the skilful double meanings, and the use of words as 'put-downs', were in a league the researcher could not match. An example of this and its social function was observed in the following incident. Ten of the regulars had gradually assembled in ones and twos early one evening outside the chip shop. As the numbers grew every passer by bar total strangers was reacted to with a greeting or a ridiculing remark. The slow arrival of the local policeman on his bike was hailed with hoots of amusement. Paddy took charge and chatted pleasantly with the policeman about the youth club and the cost of bus fares. Bob, something of an upstart, tried to get the policeman's attention by examining his bike and loudly telling a story about leading the police a dance. Paddy tolerated this for a while then moved decisively, shifting Bob to the edge, and remarking that Bob thought he was hard but he could deal with him. At this point the group had lost its cohesion with one of its members put down in front of the policeman, and it fragmented over the pavement. The policeman got back on his bike and left saying he had a few more jobs to do yet. Paddy responded rapidly that he had the perfect disguise for a burglar and the resulting burst of laughter at the policeman's expense united the group once more.

The argument is that while the central regulars who, to an outsider's view, could well have been taken as typical of the delinquent youth of the estate, had a history of fighting and tended to admire those who were hard, the physical expression of this assertiveness sprang out of their identification with the estate and the need to defend it and their position on it. This attitude, although it sometimes led them into clashes with the law, hardly seemed to merit the term delinquent or deviant. Nor did they think delinquent behaviour was particularly heroic although they condoned it. Mac, a serious delinquent by any standards, was only a peripheral and intermittent associate of the group. Bob, who had convictions for theft, burglary and indecent assault and had been sent to detention centre at only fourteen, was accepted in the group but he was not especially respected by any means. His status in the regulars appeared to be determined by his own character and behaviour and not by his record. Derek said philosophically that:

> anyone could commit a crime but whether you get caught depends more on who you are, your family.

In other words someone like Bob had little chance of getting away with anything since his two older brother had police records. Ally had only ever had minor brushes with the law, at football matches. He had weighed the pros and cons. He did not think it was worth the risk of losing one's job, possibly getting kicked out of home, and having to pay a fine or other penalty, just for the excitement of committing a crime. He said while he was at school all his friends had a meter key to steal money from the electricity and gas prepayment meters. Some of them made a lot of money this way. He never felt the urge himself. It was interesting that not only did Ally apparently not feel in any way pressured by the activities of his friends but his standing in his peer group was not affected either. Sandy had convictions but not for criminal offences. He had been to court four times for riding a motorcycle without a licence, insurance, helmet etc., and carrying passengers whilst still a learner. He and Mark had also been in trouble for shooting birds with guns for which they had no licence.

In other contexts than crime the central regulars had conventional working class standards. In one brief discussion in which the researcher almost let his 'middle class intellectual' persona break through it was made clear that the lads were patriotic, would fight for Queen and country, and disapproved of lefties, particularly 'these disarmament people'. Concern for reciprocity and fairness was a very significant feature of their social lives. This came out most clearly in the public house when rounds of drinks were being bought. Some had jobs but none earned much and there were days of the weekly cycle when some had money and others not, and other days when the position was reversed. One evening the researcher bought two rounds to Ally's one. Ally said he would equal up the pints the next time they were in the pub. He seemed to avoid the researcher for ten days then suddenly appeared and squared the accounts. The boys' attitude to work varied a good deal but in general there was a lack of aspiration. Gerald had nearly finished training to be a chef. Ally was a butcher's assistant and despite grumbles intended to stay. These were the only two with unbroken work records. Paddy had a training scheme place in photography but when it finished became unemployed. Sandy, Derek, Stewart, Mark, Jimmy and the others who had left school had spent time doing hotel kitchen work and as labourers with a demolition company. They seemed destined for intermittent unskilled employment. Sandy had left the demolition firm after a row with the foreman and had then teamed up with Paddy's father on an unofficial basis cleaning the shop windows of the estate. This suited him since he could choose his hours and also collect his giro. Bob was officially at school but since no school would take him it was the same as being unemployed apart from the money. The girls of the group had jobs as a hospital auxiliary, a stable girl, and a kitchen hand.

The central regulars then were ordinary teenagers rather than moral deviants. It was true that they paid scant regard to laws just because they were laws such as the age restrictions on drinking in public houses, the regulations for riding motorcycles or possessing guns, or the moral obligation not to take casual labour while drawing supplementary benefit. But these attitudes are widespread in society from the housewife who risks parking on yellow lines to the bigtime tax evader. These attitudes are far from being deviant, they are the norm.

There was only one aspect of their value system which showed up as supporting anything other than conventional attitudes. That was their tolerant view of other people's crimes or misdemeanours, coupled with their distrust of the police, whom they believed were out to get them given the slightest excuse. The attitudes here of the central regulars contrasted signifiantly with the attitudes expressed by the adults interviewed and with the homecentred teenagers. Streetcentred teenagers in general held views similar to the central regulars.

Police were a source of amusement, a sitting target to taunt and outwit, or at worst an unpredictable force with power to jump on you and pull you in for nothing at all just because they had nothing better to do. There were ways at getting back at them of course. Derek once gave some serious advice to a younger regular on tactics for use in the event of being picked up and placed in a police car. You kept your wits about you and you could take opportunities such as sitting on and squashing a policeman's hat left on the back seat or the ripping or crumpling of papers left around. However there were many indications that they distinguished between policemen as individuals. For example Paddy had been willing to talk goodnaturedly with the local constable when he came along on his bicycle one summer evening while they were all standing about. Others like Bob had been more ambivalent. However Paddy remarked when the policeman had gone that he knew 'exactly what he was up to' implying that he was aware that the PC was not just chatting to the boys for the pleasure of their company and that there were ulterior motives. Sandy gave three contrasting examples of police behaviour. One incident he observed took place in the Chinese take-away when a dispute over a payment arose. There were shouts and threats but he felt that the proprietor and the customer would have sorted it out but someone else called the police who came racing along, grabbed the customer, and arrested the person with him because he remonstrated that they had not ascertained the facts. That Sandy felt was typical of police behaviour when called to some incident they did not understand involving persons they did not know. They inevitably made things worse. Then there were individual policemen who deliberately provoked trouble. There was one particular detective whom several of the regulars had come into contact with. This DC would grab anyone he recognized who happened to be standing around, take them round the back somewhere, rough them up, and ask them what they were going to tell him. You just had to play along with the DC, there was nothing you could do. On the other hand the one on the bicycle was not like that at all. He really seemed to like talking to ordinary people and he remembered things about you, asked after your family, called in the neighbourhood centre, and you felt you could approach him as an equal.

The reasons for the distrust of, if not hostility to, the police in general by the regulars and most of the streetcentred youth of the estate were based on experience. On this topic however as was stated before they differed markedly from the parental generation. The high rate of reporting to police which was characteristic of the adult residents was not found among the streetcentred youth. Over a third of them said they would never report anything witnessed short of murder or a sex attack. No-one said they would report fights or property vandalism. Even those who had suffered bike thefts or had been beaten up had rarely even told their parents let alone the police. As Mac said:

132

I wouldn't report anything at all. It brings a load
of bloody hassle. Better sort it out yourself,
round Omega anyway.

In summary therefore, although the streetcentred youth of
Omega and in particular the group which regularly frequented
the centre of the estate could be said to hold certain
characteristic attitudes and views, these did not amount to
a subculture of delinquency. On the vast majority of topics
their values were utterly conventional and there was no
evidence from anything said or observed that thieving,
burgling or even fighting (unless in defence of the estate,
one's friends or oneself) were desirable let alone glorious
activities.

EFFECTS OF LABELLING

Another possible explanation of why such a high rate of
delinquency was recorded for Omega youth was that the estate
was 'labelled'. The drawbacks of labelling theory were
discussed in Chapter 1 but the material on Omega teenagers
provided another test. Evidence that labelling contributed
to the number of recorded offences committed by Omega youth
would have to show that police selected Omega for extra
attention, that patrolling police accounted for a sizeable
proportion of prosecutions, and that Omega youth responded
with increased delinquency to live up to the image. Clearly
none of these assertions was open to any kind of rigorous
proof. Nor were there comparative data on these issues from
other parts of the city.

However the teenagers of the sample provided a fairly
consistent picture in what they said and from the
researcher's observations. Teenagers (whether streetcentred
or homecentred) on the estate were familiar with the police.
While adult respondents often claimed they had not seen a
policeman on the estate in years this was not the case with
the youth. No less than eighty per cent of the males and
twenty four per cent of the females had been stopped at
least once by police, usually on suspicion only. This
practice meant the teenagers were only too aware of a local
police presence. The following examples cover a range of
situations in which a girl or boy had been stopped on Omega:

Paul had bought a radio cassette in the city one Saturday
and was walking home into the estate when a panda drew up
and a policeman questioned him about it. He felt he was
lucky that he had kept the receipt and was able to show it

to them. Ten minutes later another panda stopped him and the process was repeated.

Robert was stopped on two successive nights cycling home into the estate from work because he had no proper lights. He was sure that on the second night the police had waited especially to catch him.

Kevin had been stopped by police when he was riding his brand new bicycle round the estate. The number of the bicycle frame was checked.

Andy was walking down a main road on the estate at night with a friend both dressed in 'mod' gear. Suddenly the police drove up 'like the Sweeney', piled out and searched them with no explanation. They found nothing and let them on their way.

Rick was standing on a street corner in a group of nine or ten others when they noticed a panda cruising past and then returning and going past again. Eventually it stopped, the policeman got out and told them not to make so much noise.

Debbie was just 'standing around' on the estate when a police car stopped and asked what she was doing and where she lived. She put their interest in her down to the fact that she was wearing her Doctor Marten's boots.

Michelle (a black girl) was walking into the estate with friends after a blues night in the city when police stopped and questioned them for no apparent reason.

Each of the examples above was recounted in similar vein many times. It was not surprising therefore that there were certain broad agreements among the estate teenagers whether homecentred or streetcentred concerning police practice. Fifty five per cent stated their belief that police picked on young people from Omega more than from other places. But seventy per cent were of the opinion that police picked on particular types of young person, such as 'punks, skinheads, blacks and people in gangs' wherever they lived. And everybody was certain that police picked on persons they knew who had been in trouble before.

This belief in itself did not necessarily lead to a hostile or distrustful attitude to the police. The homecentred teenagers, despite the fact that two thirds of them had been stopped at some time by police, nevertheless all expressed a generally positive view and like the parental generation were in favour of more patrolling. Of the streetcentred teenagers only a quarter had a favourable opinion of the police. Forty per cent were quite definitely hostile:

> I hate the pigs, they pick on people because they've
> nothing else to do, they're all mad and they cause
> violence.

The rest had mixed and sometimes contradictory views
alleging discrimination and arbitrary justice while
recognising they were upholding law and order and saying
there should be more of them. Given the limitations of the
data it was possible to collect with any accuracy it
appeared that the most extremely hostile attitudes to police
were held by those boys who had been prosecuted for criminal
offences. West (1982) presented evidence that delinquents'
attitudes to police became significantly more hostile
following a conviction compared with their attitudes at an
earlier age when, according to self report, they were
already breaking the law but had not been through the court
process. The explanation could be the effects of labelling
or it might rather be explained by features of police
behaviour which caused resentment among the prosecuted
youths both during the judicial process and after. That is
what youths themselves said was the case. Mac for example
complained that once he had become known to the police:

> They pick me up now for nothing at all. They only
> have to see me to stop me. I hate them.

It was therefore likely that police did give selective
attention to Omega although it may rather have been the
disproportionate numbers of youthful punks, skinheads and
blacks who were the targets rather than the estate as such.
There was no evidence however that this attention led to the
police discovering many offences. Even with teenagers the
vast majority of offences came to police notice through the
reports of witnesses or victims. The police attention might
have hardened the attitudes of teenagers on the estate,
particularly those who had already been in trouble, and made
them more inclined to defiant acts. But it would seem
unlikely that the labelling factor was in itself the
explanation for Omega's very high rate of recorded juvenile
offending.

SITUATIONAL FACTORS

The commonsense explanation of teenage delinquency being
particularly high on Omega was given by the adult residents
interviewed. Sixty per cent put it down to 'boredom' and
'nothing to do on this estate'. Although delinquency did

not logically follow from there not being anything to do on the estate examples from Chapter 7 showed how easily ordinary pastimes such as playing football or messing about with motorbikes could cause residents to call for police intervention. The reasons for that could be classed as 'situational' arising out of the design and layout of the estate. The fact that the teenage group who frequented the youth club in the centre of the estate where there was more to do than anywhere else included several of the best known delinquents on Omega suggested 'nothing to do' was not really the key factor. The work of Baldwin and Bottoms (1976) bore this out when they studied twenty four council estates in Sheffield with wide differences in delinquency rates and found no correlation between the provision of youth club facilities and level of delinquency. On the other hand on Omega the streetcentred teenagers including the central regulars, when asked, said they were bored most of the time. A combination of boredom and opportunities to act on the environment to make something, anything, happen was the basis of Parker's (1974) theory of 'creative' delinquency which fitted the facts on Omega.

The following episodes recounted by Omega teenagers had resulted or could have resulted in police intervention. They were all typical of the delinquency which figured so greatly in police and court records and in the experience of estate residents. Some incidents just seemed to happen because no-one thought of the possible consequences.

Andy, before he had his own moped, wanted to go and see his girlfriend, and got his friend's permission to ride his. He was stopped and found not to be covered by his friend's insurance.

Two youths living near the Binghams were looking for firewood on bonfire night. They noticed some panels of fencing, bought at their own expense by the Binghams, which was leaning up against the house. They took it for their bonfire.

The Rhodes boys went over to land behind the allotments to scramble on their motorbikes. Someone called the police who caught them and took down their names and addresses.

Mark had learned from a friend that a device for lighting gas cookers could be used to clock up credits on electronic games. They used this to get free games until a warning by the owner of the premises caused Mark's father to confiscate the device.

Sandy had an air gun and in company with Mark who also had a gun he went trying to shoot pheasant on land beyond the estate owned by a country club. Sandy and Mark did not have licences. They occasionally got a pheasant this way. Sandy had been warned by the owner several times and prosecuted once.

Fighting seemed to be the only way to sort out peer group animosities.

Tony was not a boy who normally solved disagreements by fighting but he agreed to accompany a friend of his who was going round to see another youth who had been making trouble. They were talking to this youth on his doorstep when he pulled a knife and both Tony and his friend had to fight to defend themselves. They were the ones to be prosecuted.

When Anna had a dispute with another girl, whom she claimed had been 'spreading rumours' about her, the friends of both girls arranged a pitched fight on some waste ground. Anna said she 'went mad, and kicked and punched her' and someone phoned the police. Anna was fined a heavy fine.

From incidents told by the teenagers instances of criminal damage or vandalism were often a way of 'getting at' somebody. Several of the accounts of victimisations in Chapter 6 provided evidence of that. Other examples include:

Richie and his street mates annoyed one particular neighbour regularly by playing football outside his house. He caused trouble for the boys and as a result was the victim of a series of minor incidents of damage to his car culminating in sugar being put in his petrol tank.

Tracey was with a mixed group of younger teenagers who collected on the stairway of some flats to play their transistor (and probably to sniff glue). A man came out and shouted at them to go away. The next day one of the boys sprayed his parked car with paint.

Derek and Sandy were annoyed that they had not been invited to a party on their patch of the estate. Bouncers on the door made it clear they could not con their way in. Derek talked of putting a brick through the window, but Sandy said he had a better idea to pot shot through the window of the party from the safety of his own house across the way.

On the other hand some of the more serious instances of criminal damage were not personal. The targets did not however seem to be random.

Kevin said he and his friends once got into a factory yard

through a wire fence and caused a lot of damage to a number of lorries loaded with packaged products.

Roger and his mates broke into the school grounds during vacation, smashed desks, and ended up breaking a window.

Kenny, his younger brother, and a number of others were on the waste land by the railway embankment and threw bricks at passing trains. They became particularly enthusiastic in this activity when wagons transporting rows of new cars passed slowly by. It was at this point in the proceedings that the police arrived and caught some of them with bricks in their hands. Afterwards Kenny said:

> Dunno why the court took the whole thing so seriously. It was quite a laugh really.

Some incidents were more nuisance than lawbreaking but served to indicate what Parker (1974) termed the 'creativity' of some delinquency. A good story came out of the following mischief:

> Kevin and his friend sat on the wall near their house getting a great deal of amusement from watching a sequence of taxis arriving at a neighbour's house, each in turn to be told there must have been some mistake, no-one at the address had telephoned for a taxi. Eventually an irate and hysterical woman rushed out and accused the two boys of making the hoax calls from a nearby kiosk. Wide eyed with innocence they denied the charges.

Some of the central regulars particularly enjoyed teasing policemen testing the limits of how far they could go. Sandy and Bob were the two who seemed to take any opportunity of this type of provocative interaction.

> Bob was walking across the waste land when he noticed a group of police evidently looking for something or someone. He took to his heels just for the fun of the chase and led the posse of police through all the muddiest ground. Everyone was covered in dirt by the time they caught him and then he had the pleasure of messing up the police car and tramping mud through the police station. According to Bob they tried to pin a burglary on him which he had not done but failed to find any evidence.

> Sandy had precipitated a similar event. He was sitting with two mates by the chip shop when a panda car drove slowly past looking at them. They decided to trick the police into following them so they ran down the long dark road towards the edge of the estate. The police car reversed and headed down another road to cut them off but the boys had doubled back and cut through across some

waste land so that in a couple of minutes they were back where they had been sitting on the wall smoking cigarettes. Eventually the police car discovered them again and the annoyed policemen questioned them. They were able to find nothing against the youths but did reveal that they were looking for some stolen cars. Sandy was able to use this information to trick another pair of policemen later in the evening into thinking they were on the trail by looking scared and saying he did not know anything about any stolen cars, before the police had mentioned what they were looking for.

Taking the observations and accounts of teenage misdemeanours on Omega all together some were potentially harmful to other persons but most were difficult to categorise as deliberately or calculatedly criminal in intent. Yet these were the kinds of incidents repeated time after time in the police records for Omega youths.

Of course delinquency on Omega also included shoplifting, theft of bikes, cars, and the money from electricity meters, as well as some serious burglaries. The few teenagers who were involved in truly criminal activities and who did not mind talking about it, always expressed the idea of the 'legitimate target'. Shops were reckoned to be making a bomb charging high prices, the owners of bikes or cars could claim on the insurance, the electricity board would not notice the loss (delinquents did not seem to realise that the tenant usually had to pay) and so on.

But it was rather the opportunistic mischief of youths hanging around waiting for something to happen which made the delinquency rate of Omega appear to be so high. On the basis of the evidence provided by Omega teenagers it seemed that such incidents were precipitated out of social situations arising in a territorial context. The availability of youth clubs or other amenities made little difference serving only as a base or backdrop for the life of the group. Because the unsupervised teenagers were outside most of the time the social and the situational factors contributing to the likelihood of getting into some kind of trouble were always present. Racing motorbikes, giving rides to friends, playing football, listening to transistors, were all activities which could lead to adults complaining which then set the scene for more serious reprisals. The situational factors leading to fights between individuals or groups were also evident outside the house in the public life of the streets where there was gossip and rumour and confrontations.

Vandalism and criminal damage was more complex because it was neither accidental nor clearly motivated; it was opportunistic yet there was a pattern. Buttimer (1976), and Ley et al. (1974) quoted in Herbert (1982) put forward the idea of expression of territoriality as an unconscious motive in vandalism. The accounts and observations on Omega certainly fitted such an explanation. It would account for the targetting of schools, the police, the railway line cutting the estate off from the rest of the city; the victimisation of particular households, those who were seen as threatening the rights of the teenagers to occupy the public space; and the 'marking' of places frequented or 'owned' by them. The sort of incidents designed to make something happen could also be viewed in this light, that the streetcentred youth wanted to be active in their occupation of the estate and to make their presence felt.

But were the social and situational factors contributing to this opportunistic delinquency so much worse on Omega that they accounted for its exceptionally high rate? Social factors making Omega different included sheer numbers of teenagers and the extraordinary proportion of them in the population; the fact that more of them were unsupervised and streetcentred; and the labelling by police and press which assigned an image to estate teenagers. Situational factors included the design of the estate which exacerbated noise and visual nuisance and which provided few legitimate gathering places but numerous non-legitimate gathering places. A more normal demographic profile would have helped. Smaller neighbourhoods rather than one huge planned estate would have been better. More sports pitches, youth clubs and gathering places, particularly spread about the peripheral corners of the estate would have provided a focus for the streetcentred youth of the different neighbourhoods, and reduced the revenge element in vandalism.

Apart from this there was no remedy for the opportunistic creative delinquency of Omega except to play it cool, be tolerant and refuse to brand normal energetic outgoing youths as delinquent. For it had to be expected that unskilled, uneducated, economically disadvantaged youths whose lives were lived outside the home until they married, were going to go through a stage of asserting themselves within and between their social groups, and were going to express their presence and their identity in relation to the territory they occupied; and were going to do this in ways which strictly speaking contravened laws and regulations and caused breaches of the peace and annoyance to adult residents; and that the greater the concentration of this type of youth in any one place, the worse these problems would seem to be; and that the damage and the nuisance factors would be aggravated by housing design, structure and density, and by residential layout which promoted visibility and audibility of others. It required local, friendly police on the patch, on the beat; the ones who could accept a lot of mickeytaking, and did not feel an immediate urge to display their authority and power; who knew by experience who were the lads who were basically well intentioned and those who were deliberate lawbreakers. Such police were not the ones who roughly stopped and searched kids hanging around or walking home at night nor the ones who raced up in response to a call and, by arresting all and sundry, dangerously escalated group hostilities. Residents needed to learn not to call the police at every little disturbance of the peace, so long as no really serious harm was done, and the uninvolved passer by was not threatened.

And if one says in answer to this that despite all the 'excuses', the theme of many chapters of this report so far has been the right of residents to live without harassment and to expect the statutory services to do their best to guarantee their peaceful enjoyment of their homes, then it should be remembered that interviews with the adults in the household sample did not identify teenagers as the chief soure of actual nuisance or harassment. Neighbours were far more likely to cast a longterm blight on people's lives than teenage noise or stolen cars. What did bother respondents was the reputation they believed the teenagers caused the estate to have; and the fear that at school or in the streets their own children would get into trouble by being in the wrong company. This reputation could only be got rid of if police, officials and respectable residents stopped over-reacting to teenage misdemeanours and got together to provide more places on the estate which teenagers could regard as their own, to scramble, to play football, to play music, to regard as their territory.

And as a footnote to the point being made it might be salutory to compare the examples of 'delinquency' quoted earlier with two incidents of really serious, even dangerous, criminal damage reported in the papers during the period of the study. The first concerned the shooting down of a hot air balloon which was operating a pleasure trip by peppering it with shotgun pellets. The second concerned damage to a room in a public house where food was smeared on walls, plates of foot were tipped into the carpet, wine bottles were smashed against furniture, curtains were ripped

141

from rails, the carpets were covered with vomit, and the landlord faced with a bill of nearly £1,000 in repairs. The first offence was perpetrated by a group of lords and viscounts on a grouse moor in Yorkshire and resulted in no prosecutions. The second offence was the work of a group of Cambridge undergraduates who were taken to court but acquitted since their parents had immediately paid up the cost of repairing the damage to the victimised landlord.

10 The traders

There were twenty four commercial trading premises on the estate (excluding the kind of unofficial businesses some individuals ran from home like car repairs or decorating). Among the range of shops were a centrally placed small supermarket and three general grocery stores catering for more peripheral parts of the estate; a wool shop, an ironmonger, a butcher, a greengrocer, two post offices combined with newsagents and confectioners, a bakery, and a chemist.   There were services such as a launderette, a hairdresser, a cleaner's and a petrol station.   There was a bookmaker's, two take-aways and two public houses. All these traders shared one common characteristic, that their business was local since nobody passed through Omega to get anywhere else and nobody visited unless they had friends or relatives living there.

Their experience of life on Omega was however coloured by their differences: whether they opened during the day or only lunchtimes and evenings; whether their trade was quiet like the wool shop or hectic like sweet shops or newsagents; whether the owners or managers themselves lived on the estate or elswhere in the city; whether the premises were part of a company chain like the chemist and newsagents or a small family business like the butcher or corner shops. The above factors were no doubt implicated in their vulnerability to victimisation and crime a topic on which most of the traders had plenty to say. Almost all of the seventeen shops claimed shoplifting was a major problem the exceptions being the wool shop with rarely more than one customer at a time, and the butcher and the bakery where the goods were all under glass. It was not possible to know objectively whether the shoplifting rate was higher on Omega than on Chalkbury or elsewhere, although some shopkeepers declared it was worse than any other area in which they had run a business. Probably the rate was high if for no other reason than the preponderance of children, said to be the chief culprits. For the supermarket, the various corner shops, and the newsagents and confectioners, shoplifting seemed to present a continual nightmare.

Only two of the shops had a policy of always calling the police and going for a prosecution of someone caught shoplifting. They, the central newsagent and tobacconist and the chemist, were members of a chain of such shops and therefore it was company policy rather than a personal decision. The newsagent's manager said:

> Just can't estimate the shoplifting loss, mostly petty, but every single case we tell the police and we prosecute whenever possible, it's a deterrent. The police always stress to us the benefits of prosecuting, you may be helping someone who's shoplifting as a cry for help.

Only the previous week they had called the police to deal with two children, who had been caught before, but who were under ten years old, the age at which prosecution is possible:

> Nothing could be done of course, they were under age, but the police said they would go to their parents. We would prosecute if we could, yes, every time as a deterrent.

The manageress of the chemist's had the same policy and had even reported to the police some particular children whom she suspected but had never caught redhanded.

But these two shops were the exceptions among shops for the same reason indicated, that their livelihood did not entirely depend on the support and goodwill of the local people. The extent of this dependence was illustrated in the case of some of the other shops who took a different approach to shoplifters. The owners of a corner shop in the older part of the estate were one example. They had been there only a year and had learned a lot in the time:

We don't trust any of the kids now, we used to, like my husband caught one little girl, he just warned her, but he didn't ban her from the shop, then she came back and did it again. He went to the parents but there was no remorse. When we first opened the shop we were very naive, didn't even cover the sweets but we've learned our lesson now.

This couple had never once called the police:

We're afraid of backlash, afraid of trouble. They'd come back and damage the place, break the window or something.

The same family complained that neighbours and other children in their children's school obviously thought that because they had a shop they must be well off when this was not so. Their trade suffered because most people went to the city supermarkets:

Here's just for when they run out of something, send the kids here for the smallest size of whatever it is they've run out of, so of course it seems dear, larger sizes are always cheaper, so they think we're trying to rip them off. And the kids keep 10p for themselves each time so the parents think we're even dearer than we are. We're the same people as them, used to live in the flats, got off our backsides, but they all think you're loaded if you have a shop, but it's never made a profit, made a loss last year.

The fear of the local community felt by these shopkeepers led to them taking no action in a blatant case of theft. The wife recounted:

Three coloured boys just walked in and emptied the fridge of pies and pasties. I couldn't stop them and they just made off up the street.

A similar attitude was expressed by another corner shop:

It's a problem anywhere but it's worse here. We've never prosecuted and we've only ever banned three of them from the shop. We always deal with it ourselves, never called the police. If it's kids, we have to decide whether to go and see their parents or not. Don't want to make too much fuss as this causes illfeeling. It's this 'them and us' attitude, don't want to aggravate it without cause. I don't know if one is allowed to say it but the coloured people are very touchy, wouldn't like to give them any cause to start trouble with us.

The owner of another local store towards the north of the estate was an Asian who had bought the business only three months earlier with the help of relatives in the city. He was already thinking he had made a big mistake. He claimed the previous owner (who had stayed only eighteen months) had 'cooked the books to make it look as though the shop was doing well'. The Asian was apparently appalled more than any of the English shopkeepers by the character of the estate:

> I don't understand this estate. I've lived in England twenty five years and known many other council estates but never one like this, the children especially, I don't understand them. The people are not very nice, there's too much thieving, problems every day. I lose £15 to £20 a day from shoplifting. I don't want to do anything like call the police because I'd be worried that it would cause too much trouble, also because I'm black, they might come back and break a window. It's not worth while when you're trying to build a business.

He had already had some nasty experiences attempting to deal with things himself:

> I caught two girls shoplifting, only one had the stuff on her. So I sent the other one to tell her friend's mother I wanted to speak to her. Well she came and she was angry, saying why had I sent for her and not for the other girl's mother? She shouted all kinds of abuse at me, as if I'd made it up, and said she'd never use the shop again. I said that's up to you, I can't afford £3 to £4 worth of thefts by your daughter. I do my best to keep people happy, I stay open till 6 p.m. seven days a week and still they're not happy.

The Asian's customers had clearly pulled every trick they knew since he had taken over the store:

> I've had three bad cheques since I've been here, with the wrong address on them so you can't find the people, children steal the change for themselves and then the parents come round and say they've been shortchanged and how do I prove it? Two or three times a day this happens.

He too felt the 'them and us' feeling towards shop-keepers, mentioned by some of the other small store-keepers:

> They take it out on the shopkeeper. There's more and more on the dole, less and less money, and prices going up and up, they take it out on the

shopkeeper. They don't understand we can't help it, it's the Government. I'd like to keep the prices down but I can't. I only want to make a living and help people. But I'm selling up if I get any opportunity.

The worst aspect of all this for the family shops was not so much the victimisation itself but the lack of being able to take firm steps for fear of losing business. The other newsagent's on the northern side of the estate and the central supermarket were run by managers and, as company businesses with large turnovers, they were not so vulnerable. Nonetheless they did not have an automatic prosecution policy. The newsagent manager said:

The shoplifting's heavy. You've got to really watch them. It's eighty per cent children. Normally, we get in touch with the parents and sometimes report them to the school. If it's bad enough we ban them from the shop. There's certain kids and adults we look out for and if known kids come in and don't want to buy anything we ask them to leave. But we have to be careful other customers don't take exception to this. Like with the darkies, they're very easily offended and take the hump. We've always made a point of being nice and friendly and establishing a good relationship. We would prosecute if it was persistent but it's not worth calling the police for children. The police aren't interested and it's bad for trade. Never had the problem in Southall, the Asians don't cause problems not like the Jamaicans. Mind you, the girls from the convent were worst.

The manager also had problems with unpaid paper bills:

They up and leave their bills unpaid. Today, a £42 bill and the people have just cleared off. There's many with bills of £15 or £16. We threaten them with court action but they know it isn't worth our while for these amounts. And if we go round to the house we're likely to get attacked. Sometimes a social worker comes and says she'll see the bill's paid off £1 a week but it's never worked yet. But you could damage the business if someone you were heavy handed with started spreading it about. I just have to wait till there's a vacancy for a manager elsewhere, definitely off Omega. This area is worse than my previous place in the docklands of London.

147

The central supermarket had a firm policy. The manager was interviewed standing in the middle of the shop in view of the till with his eyes constantly darting this way and that:

> It's kids all the time, every day. The staff know them all. We're out to get them. If we catch them they get kicked out, the stuff taken off them, and then they're banned from the shop. If they're very young we've been to see the parents or written. If it's old folk it may not be deliberate. We have a quiet word but if we think it is, we ban them too. Waste of time bringing police into it, all that happens is they're warned or if they go to court they're fined and they're back at it soon enough. Also, I have to spend a day in court when I could be here stopping thieves.

This supermarket had been twenty five years on the estate, was the only large selfservice shop, was in the central precinct, and was not teetering like the smaller local businesses between profit and loss. It was something of an institution on the estate and the manager himself had been there for thirteen years. The supermarket could afford to be vigilant and strict with shoplifters.

All but two of the shops could recall at least one break-in in recent years and four serious burglaries had taken place in the year prior to the interviews. The chemist's and the supermarket had lost money and stock by burglars breaking into the backs of the premises. In both cases the burglars were teenage boys from the estate. It was the impression of the butcher on Omega that the seriousness and the professionalism of burglaries was increasing. After twenty years of relatively trouble-free trading he had suffered four break-ins during the last few months. He had responded to the first break-in which had been to his back yard deepfreeze by calling in a security firm who put in special locks and alarms. The security had foiled the next attempt but since then the burglars had changed their tactics and had broken into the shop itself, smashed the locks on the fridges and taken £600 of meat. The butcher linked his troubles with the recession and unemployment:

> They're a direct response to a very tight money situation, and the high prices, people are really feeling the pinch.

The chip shop also felt that the situation was deteriorating. It was a longstanding family business with another branch in the city centre. It had been there for over fifteen years and the family had just taken out a new fifteen year lease. The first ten years had been uneventful but over the last five years there had been two break-ins to get at the safe and four incidents of a door or window smashed. The premises now had bars on all the windows except the main front one visible from the street.

The traders who opened evenings and weekends had problems of a rather different kind, with troublemaking customers. There seemed to be a common policy on this that the police would not be called unless things were really out of control. The chip shop owner said:

> You get to know most of the lads and you can humour or ignore them. We know the ones that are just out to start something, they'll come over the counter to get you. We have to call the police then, but we don't really want to catch them. It's the only thing to make them go away. Police tend to be slow in coming to calls but that's probably because if I have to ring them it's at their busiest time around 11 o'clock on a Saturday. Once I rang and the sergeant told me it would be at least half an hour because the shifts were changing.

The Chinese take-away had changed hands after a bad brawl which got into the papers and the new Chinese owners had been there just over a year:

> We've had a lot of trouble with customers, but we're getting to know them now and I think it's getting better now. They're usually drunk and they argue about paying, saying they gave you a £5 note. Some of them do it deliberately, they take the meal, and eat it, and then come back and say it was the meal for three instead of four, or something was bad. Sometimes to stop trouble we give them £1 back, but it they won't go away we have to call the police, just to get them removed. The police believe us of course but can't get the money back for us. We don't want any trouble so we have never gone to court. A drunk just sat there once and wouldn't go and we wanted to close the shop up. We called the police and he decided to go but he smashed the window in as he left. But we made no charges, want no trouble.

The landlords of both the public houses were very unforthcoming and evasive when the subject of trouble and victimization came up. Both couples had been on the estate less than two years and presumably had a vested interest in keeping the reputation of the pub under them a good one.

The only reference to the possible stresses intrinsic in the job was when one of the landlords said they did a 'pub swap' to come to the estate because 'the previous landlord couldn't handle it'. Both landlords omitted to mention incidents of brawls involving the police being called to the pub which were on record or told to us by other respondents. Taken altogether however it would seem that the public houses shared the same problems as the take-aways, and dealt with them in the same way, informally if possible, resorting to the police if someone would not go away but not prosecuting. The betting shop manager stated much the same.

The attitude of the traders to harassment, damage or even criminal offences was therefore very different from that found among the residential population. Traders dealt with matters themselves in a low key fashion or simply put up with a lot of trouble and losses because of fear of losing business. They were in general also very friendly with the police but showed no signs of using them as weapons in hostile confrontations in the way described for some of the residents in Chapter 6. They saw the police as the best way to prevent trouble in the first place. Most of them stated they would like to see more local 'bobbies' getting to know people. This was seen as a strategy that would pay off. The butcher spoke for others when he said:

> We definitely need more of them strolling about. Panda cars are no use in preventing or in catching them. But things may be improving. A week ago, a young PC came into the shop and said I'm Chris something, your local bobby, have you any problems? Now, that's really good.

The chip shop owner said:

> They do a very good job but there should be more of the walking type, can get to know the regulars then they have more chance of catching them when they do something.

The Chinese take-away owner sensibly said that if they got out of their panda cars they would learn the times of the day and week when trouble could be prevented by a policeman being there.

However despite the commonsense and realism of the traders on Omega the problems associated with the estate could not be overlooked particularly by those premises which were centrally placed or were by their nature targets for thefts, vandalism or brawls. It was significant that nearly half the estate shops, one of the take-aways and both the public

150

houses had changed hands in the last two years. However all
the remainder had been under the present ownership or
management for at least five years, most as long as ten,
fifteen or more years. It looked as though if a trader
could survive the first two years he dug in, became accepted
and began to reap the benefits. The same phenomenon was of
course found with ordinary residents that the longer they
had lived on Omega the more satisfied they were and the less
likely they would want to move (Chapter 11). All the
longstanding traders, except for the greengrocer, said that
business was good and they intended to stay. These included
the shops in the central precinct which had no direct
competition such as the baker, the post office and
newsagent, the launderette, the hairdresser, the butcher,
the chip shop and so on. The little general stores in the
corners of the estate had the biggest problems making ends
meet and were the shops most likely to have changed hands in
the past two years. As one of the shopkeepers quoted above
indicated, people tended to come to his shop only when they
had run out of something, not to do their main weekly
shopping, since his prices could not compete with the
central city supermarkets. Probably of more significance
however was the fact that the businesses where the ownership
or management kept changing were the ones most vulnerable to
'trouble', whether in the form of attracting confrontations
and brawls as with the take-away or public houses or because
they were afraid of reprisals if they reported thieves to
the police.

A noticeable feature of the conversations of the traders
was that not one of them seemed to feel part of the estate
life even though two thirds of them lived on the estate in
accommodation attached to the premises or flats above the
precinct shops. There was an 'us and them' feeling well
expressed by the couple who ran one of the struggling local
stores:

> We've never been happy with the general attitude,
> people here think you're making a fat living out of
> them. Like last week our son didn't have the right
> felt tip pen at school and the teacher said there's
> no excuse for you is there, you've got a shop,
> things like that. We're the same people as them,
> used to live in the flats, got off our backsides.

At a different level the well off well educated Asian owner
of the launderette said he was disillusioned by the response
of the community centre organisers and members. When he
first arrived he had offered to help in all kinds of ways
and provided a hot dog stall and barbecue for the annual

fete which had been very successful and raised a lot of money:

> They never thanked me, never followed it up, never asked me again, though I would have been happy to help but I was never approached. I felt very disillusioned. They're very cliquish over there.

In the context of this conversation he seemed to be attributing the standoffishness of the community centre organisers to the fact that he was a trader rather than to the possibility of a racial barrier. On that issue he was in fact adamant that:

> There's a good racial mix here, we're all well integrated.

The launderette owner said he liked the estate however, but on that point he was in a small minority amongst the traders. All but four of them said they disliked the estate as a place, disliked the people or both. The woolshop lady was exceptional in her view:

> It's a beautiful place, lovely houses, good buses and nice people.

The rest included those with successful or unsuccessful businesses, those who had been there a long time or a short time, those who lived on the estate or lived elsewhere. It might have been the feeling that ordinary residents regarded them as different, as predators almost, that coloured their vision of Omega. Typical of the traders were the following comments:

> It's monotonous, it's drab, it's too big, it's too expensive to keep taking the bus to the town so everybody feels trapped.

> There's no facilities for the kids and there's one hell of a lot of kids, nowhere to go except the pubs and you can't let them in.

> Oh the estate's all right, quite wellplanned, it's the people they put here. It's all the children, when they get together, you can't help it, there'll be trouble. And parents don't bother, they haven't the same standards these days.

> They dump problem families here of course, social services would tell you. It's been a conscious decision and it's very wrong.

> There's some very odd people here and they planned it for the coons didn't they? It's them giving the

152

place a bad name. I think there's something about this place though that gives people problems. As soon as we came to live here my marriage broke up and it happens to a lot of people.

In fact no fewer than ten of the twenty four traders interviewed specifically mentioned the problem of blacks, coons, darkies, coloureds and ghettoes as a reason for the estate being undesirable (yet it must be remembered that West Indians made up less than ten per cent of the population and there were very few Asians indeed). Similar remarks were made by a quarter of the ordinary residents (Chapter 11) but it was a recurring and dominant theme amongst traders. Did traders simply express their feelings more freely than residents? Was this simply a way of distancing themselves from the estate? Or did their experiences with the public force the 'problem' to their attention? Certainly common to many of the traders was the feeling that you had to be especially careful with black customers because as a newsagent was quoted as saying earlier:

They're very easily offended and take the hump.

Similarly a small grocery proprietor said:

The coloured people are very touchy, wouldn't like to give them any cause to start trouble with us.

Another corner shop said the same:

They think because they're black and got no dads or whatever nobody can do anything to them. We could easily have trouble if we said the wrong thing to the wrong people.

The Asian shopkeeper, also quoted earlier, felt the same fear in reverse:

I don't want to do anything like call the police . . . . because I'm black, they might come back and break a window.

But the Chinese take-away proprietor although faced with plenty of problems was delightfully optimistic in his outlook maybe because of his insulated life in a large Chinese family or because of the contrast Omega afforded to his previous area of business in a run down area of a northern city:

Here is everything people need, a health centre, a community hall and plenty of shops. The only thing is there are too many boys without a job and they get into trouble. I say to my son you must study

153

hard and then you get a good job. But he's lazy and
he watches TV and he goes into town. The Government
should train all boys to do a job. And then we can
all live peacefully together.

11 On the bright side

The emphasis of preceding chapters has been on the problems that beset residents of Omega, problems which seemed to originate from the characteristics of the estate itself. It is however important to redress the balance somewhat by reminding readers that the majority of people talked to on Omega were happy to live on the estate. While as many as forty four per cent of respondents had not chosen to come to live on the estate in the first place, once settled there, half of those reluctant tenants wanted to stay put. Overall just over two thirds of those interviewed were happy to live in the area and had no intention of trying to move anywhere else. Everyone agreed there were problems associated with living on the estate but only a minority were really unhappy there. The characteristics of the majority, the non-complaining settled residents, were as diverse as those for the population as a whole but it was possible to list some of the factors clearly associated with being content. Certain types of residents were found to have a much higher than average probability of satisfaction, the average being sixty eight per cent. Those who expressed more than average contentment with being on Omega are shown in Table 3. Some of the factors listed in the Table were more or less chance outcomes of the allocation process such as 'living in the western half' which contained lower density housing, with more houses and fewer flats or maisonettes. 'Liking the dwelling' had a subjective element but on the other hand

Table 3

Characteristics of satisfied residents

Characteristic	Percentage expressing satisfaction with estate
Those who liked their house or flat and were happy with their immediate neighbourhood	98%
Regular users of at least one of the recreational amenities on the estate such as a public house or the community centre	89%
Those with relatives of the woman living on the estate or close by	86%
Those who chose Omega in the first place	86%
Those happy with their immediate neighbourhood	86%
Those resident more than fifteen years on Omega	84%
Those with no troublesome neighbours	83%
Those who liked their house or flat	82%
Those who felt that all the neighbours were friendly	82%
Those who said they had never been the victim of an offence or nuisance while on the estate	82%
Those who had contacted only one agency or none at all over recent years	82%
Those who counted three or more friends among their neighbours	80%
Those who said they were friendly with next door neighbours only, but did not know the others at all	79%
Those who socialised with their neighbours	78%
Those who felt the bad reputation of estate was created by outside infuences such as the media	77%
The retired, or couples with grown-up children	75%
Those families where the head was a skilled (as opposed to unskilled or white collar) worker in employment	75%
Those who lived in the western half of the estate.	74%
Average of all respondents	68%

some designs of house and maisonette and flat were deservedly unpopular and led to the same complaints over and over again, so to some extent that was also the luck of the allocation draw. Again, 'having troublesome neighbours' could be seen as either subjective or objective; between the lines of some respondents' stories could be read the implication of a pot and kettle situation, but there was no doubt that, in some streets, one troublesome household made life unpleasant for just about everyone else. The haphazard nature of the allocation process therefore was the single largest factor deciding where a family taking up a tenancy on the estate lived, in what kind of dwelling and whether their neighbours would cause trouble.

The other factors were determined more by the families themselves or their circumstances. One of the most significant was the presence on the estate of wife's relatives (strangely enough having husband's relatives close by seemed to have no effect on level of satisfaction). Women with relatives on Omega tended to attribute the bad reputation to external labelling rather than to deviant elements on the estate itself. The presence of relatives frequently provided an interest, a readymade social life, and practical support. And when people were content in their personal circumstances the wider social setting became less important.

In view of the above it was encouraging to find that as many as forty two per cent of respondent households had matrilineal relatives living on the estate with whom they were in regular contact. This indicated that despite the strict rules of the housing allocation system women were managing gradually to reconstruct the matrilocal kin networks which contributed so much to the stability of older generations of working class communities. It could however be the case that this goal was rather easier to achieve on an unpopular high turnover estate such as Omega than it would have been on the well thought of estates which had rare vacancies. It is not a widespread policy for housing authorities to give official weighting to an application for a tenancy on a particular estate to persons who have relatives there. The GLC however, until 1982, encouraged a policy whereby a special quota of housing stock was retained to offer to the children of tenants who married and wanted to remain on the same estate. They were forced to abandon the system in some boroughs because, with a severe housing shortage and in a situation where the majority of homeless families were recent immigrants, the policy was felt to be discriminatory. The problem of course was the housing shortage rather than the policy itself which would have worked for the benefit of immigrants as well as natives, once they were established on an estate; indeed a spokesman for the immigrants made it clear they supported concentration rather than dispersal of immigrant groups. There is therefore no reason why other authorities should not bring in positive weighting for relatives of existing tenants. All the evidence of twentieth century sociology points to the positive influence of localised kinship networks on the quality, interest and stabiity of human social life.

Most of the characteristics of the satisfied residents were undoubtedly typical of satisfied residents on any public housing estate. However Omega had been built originally for families with children so it was important to note that the highest proportion of contented residents was to be found amongst the retired and couples with grownup children. This underlined the message of Chapter 7 that Omega was a particularly unpopular place in which to bring up children. Since the original planners intended the opposite, and since the earlier chapter indicated some of the practical reasons why families with young and school age children experienced problems, one can only hope that future planners will do things better.

Another characteristic of satisfied residents should be mentioned that they tended to be users of local recreational amenities. Overall slightly less than a third of adult respondents regularly attended even one of the various social amenities on the estate such as either of the public houses, the community centre, or some sporting or special interest club or association. But amongst those households where one or more adult members did join in some estate recreational activity there was a marked degree of satisfaction with living on the estate. As with any correlation of social factors it was not possible to be certain of the direction of cause and effect or to know whether both factors had some other cause in common. People who did not frequent the public houses or community centre were consistent in condemning the atmosphere and the type of person who went there. Half of these nonparticipants visited public houses, community centres or clubs in other areas of the city. But the other half had very little or no recreation outside the house at all. There were on Omega social, attitudinal and racial divisions among the residents just as there are in most areas and, from what respondents said, and from observation, it was plain that certain groups had 'taken over' the different available meeting places such as the bars of the public houses or the rooms of the community centre. With an adult population of around six thousand this left a lot of individuals who did not share the ideas and interests of the groups identified with these places, with nowhere on the estate where they could casually socialise. Community centres and pubs with a fairly fixed, stable clientele who do not cater for passing visitors are always open to the criticism of being dominated by a particular clique. On Omega this problem was accentuated because there were no other places for adults to go so it was likely that if new facilities were built they would have a ready clientele and would also make the estate a happier place by increasing the choices available to the residents.

The concept of natural divisions and groups within the estate population with differing social needs, leads to a consideration of relations between the coloured immigrant residents of Omega and their white neighbours. This topic has already been touched on in previous chapters but is worth some elaboration at this point. Racial issues have not been highlighted in this report since it could not be said that racial disharmony was observed nor was it frequently commented upon in interviews with residents. As of the early eighties a race problem was not one of the major problems of Omega.

Around nine per cent of the population on the estate was New Commonwealth in ethnic origin, only a little higher than the city average of seven per cent. Coloured immigrants were not however spread evenly throughout the residential areas of the city and Omega had a higher proportion of West Indian families than any other city ward. Inner city areas contained the highest proportion of immigrants in general, one ward in particular had fifteen per cent of its population (and twenty seven per cent of its children) of New Commonwealth origin, but the majority in this case were Indians or Pakistanis. It was rare to see an Asian face on Omega. One of the city councillors on the housing committee commented that it was his hypothesis that at an immigrant level of around ten per cent there would be no problems, but that the level should not be allowed to get much above that. The policy implication of his remark was that some care would be taken to make sure that coloured immigrants were distributed fairly evenly as far as local authority housing estates were concerned. The inner city immigrant areas were predominantly owner occupied old houses and so the council had no control over the population composition there.

Whatever the reason and whether the councillor's

hypothesis was correct or not it was the case that the study of Omega revealed no allegations or rumours of systematic racial harassment, or complaints of racial discrimination (except with regard to the police), nor was racial tension sensed or observed. Nor were stories on any of these topics given the treatment by the local gutter press which itself was a good indicator of the murkier elements waiting to be churned up from time to time.

One event which took place during the period of the study illustrated the atmosphere of racial tolerance on Omega estate. A young black boy had died suddenly and, on the day of the funeral, which was held in the church on the estate, it seemed that the entire West Indian population of the Midlands converged on Omega in large old cars, which caused tremendous traffic jams and parking problems in all the roads leading into and through the estate. Thousands of black people milled around all over the pavements and on to the roads slowly converging on the church from all directions. All round the periphery and weaving in and out of the darkfaced masses were the white people going about their ordinary business, doing their shopping, waiting for the jammed up buses, pushing prams and so on. Two different worlds, not interfering with each other, barely noticing each other in fact.

Nevertheless it should be recognized that a quarter of the white respondents made some spontaneous comment indicating racial prejudice and a derogatory attitude to the black population in general. Frequently however disclaimer remarks were made making exceptions of particular black persons, such as neighbours they got on well with, or colleagues at work, or friends of the children. These expressive statements could be interpreted in different ways: either that there was in fact an undercurrent of hostility to the black immigrant population which, given particular precipitating circumstances (say, for the sake of example, the rape of a white woman by a black man, or allegations in the media of immigrants jumping the housing queue, or taking white people's jobs), could spark off racial troubles; or alternatively that the white ninety per cent of the population of the estate, through their acquaintance with the ten per cent as neighbours or workmates, were in the process of acquiring tolerance in practice while, in some cases, holding conditioned prejudiced attitudes in theory. The second is the most optimistic interpretation and was supported by the fact that the children and young people on Omega appeared to mix without tension.

The councillor however could still have been right in his
hunch that there was a threshold of concentration of
coloured immigrants in any residential area, above which the
white population would become anxious and hostile.
Certainly white respondents from one road in the south
central part of the estate which had at the time more than
the average number of black families living there, were
amongst the most hostile. However in that instance there
was no doubt that two of the West Indian families complained
of really were noisy and let their children run wild,
behaviour which, as we saw earlier in Chapter 5, led to
hostility even when white neighbours were the culprits. The
danger was of course that when black families caused trouble
there was a tendency for whites to generalise and to blame
the fact that they were black rather than recognise that one
particular family had specific undesirable characteristics
which might not apply to other black families. Signs that
white residents were, through experience and contact,
working through this tendency to generalize, towards an
understanding of the individuality of West Indians were
present in some of the quoted opinions below. Mr. and
Mrs. Sawyer lived on the road which had an unusually high
proportion of black families and showed their apprehension.
Mr. Sawyer said:

> All the wives are on tranquillisers for their
> nerves. It'll be all black here soon. It's not a
> case of racialism, but the blacks accept these sort
> of conditions, they just want a roof over their head
> at the end of the day, they're not interested in
> their homes so they don't care what the place is
> like. Every time a white family moves out, it's
> blacks move in. All round here will be a coloured
> persons' estate in a couple of years, a ghetto, like
> in America. Mind you, they're friendlier than the
> whites in some ways, always say 'hello', which is
> more than the white ones do.

And although the Sawyers had suffered damage to their car
and windows from children of one of the black families
Mrs. Sawyer commented approvingly:

> Some of the black parents though are very strict
> with their kids, and give them a good thumping when
> they do wrong.

Mr. and Mrs. Donaldson, on the same street, have already
been described in detail because they had very great trouble
from an antisocial white family living next door to them.
They also had suffered from the same petty damage and

annoyance caused by one particular family of black children and from this they tended to draw generalisations. Mr. Donaldson, for example, said:

> Too many bloody wogs in this street, we have trouble with their children.

Mrs. Donaldson was less prepared to lump them altogether and said:

> One woman across the road is really quite decent, very nice, but she's the only one. I think the others hate the whites.

And Mr. Donaldson referred as did other respondents to the question of allocation policy:

> I understood they were only allowed to have one in each street. Yet we've four round here at the moment and at one time there was seven.

The same street had organised a petition against one of the black families who had caused a lot of illfeeling by their noisy parties going on into the early hours. Mrs. Mulpepper had spoken her mind to a housing official who had come to investigate the situation:

> He said was it because they were black that caused the trouble. I said to this posh man I bet there aren't many coloured families having allnight parties where you live. But it's not because they're coloured that they cause trouble, it's the way they live. If white families did the same I'd say they were a nuisance as well. There's only two coloured families on our side now and they're both very nice. The awful ones come and go because nobody wants to have them as neighbours.

In fact there were few respondents who showed a totally undiscriminating negative attitude towards the West Indian minority. Mr. Morgan was one of the few although (perhaps because) he lived in a street which had no black tenants. He blamed everything onto them:

> All the bother comes from the coloured population. They roam around in little gangs, it was all coloureds that robbed the milkman all the time. The police are scared stiff of them.

A number of respondents had confused even conflicting views which, it could be argued, showed that tolerance was increasing with familiarity. Mr. Overton showed some understanding of both sides of the problem but also felt

162

threatened and had no answers:

> I seriously believe that they're using Omega as an experiment in black-white integration, but it hasn't worked. There's too high a pecentage of them and because there's so many of them they're a community on their own, they're not integrated. It's a major problem, we try to integrate people into the British way of life and then we swamp their culture without looking at it. We only notice it when it interferes with our own lives, wild parties and all that, and we don't understand it's their whole way of life that's different. It would be better if we relieved the pressure to integrate and respected their own way of life.

At this point it was not clear what the 'problem' was, integration or lack of it. But it was evident later that Mr. Overton feared the black culture would become dominant on Omega because officialdom was involved in positive discrimination in their favour:

> Blacks get more help with jobs and houses because the council have to prove they're not discriminating against them, and a black family round here owed £2,000 in rent arrears but a white family owed £400 got threatened with eviction. It's going to be a black ghetto here and there'll be an explosion within fifteen years.

This man and others were expressing fears that gradually there would be more and more West Indian immigrant families until they were in a majority. The fears were not inherent in the contemporary situation but of a threat seen as being in the future which went to support the councillor's ten per cent household hypothesis.

At this threshold level however as it was in the early eighties the main impression was of mutual tolerance. While the whites called the blacks uncomplimentary names in private there was no overt signs of racial tension. Some white respondents had a very positive attitude, based on their own experience with black neighbours. One young couple, the Liffeys said:

> It's like any housing estate with lots of children, lots of immigrants and lots of Scots. Of course the folklore is that all the trouble is caused by the West Indian and the Scots, fighting mostly. But the blacks, once you get to know them, they're not hostile at all, not at all threatening.

163

The Jordans had black nextdoor neighbours. Mrs. Jordan admitted:

> Much to our surprise we find them very nice. We're on very good terms.

Their neighbours had chosen their tenancy well, the Jordans were themselves great party-givers. Mr. and Mrs. Sumner wanted to move from Omega but not because of the immigrants. Mrs. Sumner said:

> It's a good place in many ways. For one thing you find the coloured people are very integrated. We've got some very pleasant coloured friends down the road.

The tolerance was happily also experienced by the black respondents in the sample none of whom complained about discriminatory or harassing behaviour by white residents. Ms. Redder, a white woman who had been married to a West Indian man, had had 'Wogs go home' written on the garage wall by children when the family first moved in but she said:

> We've never had any trouble with the parents, only the kids. But they're a bit older now and don't do it anymore.

Mr. and Mrs. Jones, a retired Jamaican couple, said:

> We've had no trouble at all, no fault with this place, we're happy here. We're the only coloured in this block but they always ask me how my husband is, if they don't see him. They say hello, and is he well, nothing much more, friendly, that type of friendly.

Mr. and Mr. Brewster, also West Indians, who had raised six children on the estate, were the most forthcoming on the topic. They were among the first tenants on the estate and felt that things from their point of view had been getting better over the years:

> The estate is pretty good now. Since the new houses were built there's more of a mixture of black and white and it makes the place more tolerant. There's only one family that keeps themselves to themselves. All the others talk. The English type of friendly, you know, hello, and it's a cold day, not what we call friendly but they don't mean to offend you.

The Brewsters had a good relationship with their immediate (white) neighbours to whom they lent tools and Mr. Brewster helped with car repairs. But he was aware of the wider implications for black people in a troubled economic climate and said shrewdly:

> When Thatcher is finished with us there'll be nothing. Shutting down schools, no hospitals, the old people and the kids suffering, then they'll turn round and blame the blacks for everything.

Thus among both black and white respondents from those who had considered the questions came a similar message, that race relations were currently alright on the estate; that by and large black families who made themselves a nuisance were treated in the same way as the larger number of white families who were antisocial in their habits; that the two ethnic groups coexisted rather than mixed socially, with exceptions; that both groups maintained the 'English type' of friendly interaction whenever neighbours met; but that both groups harboured fears that the situation could change for the worse in certain circumstances, perhaps if the proportion of black households increased or the economic situation deteriorated further.

Another minority group who in society at large are often at a disadvantage was the elderly. But on Omega they were a relatively contented and well looked after group of residents. The majority lived in purpose-built flats; they were more likely than average to have relatives, usually their married children, living on the estate; and they were the least likely category to be victimised in any way either by vandalism, property theft or burglaries. More than that however there was a well organised voluntary service called 'Good Neighbours' which made a big difference to their lives. This had been an initiative in the seventies by the vicar and his wife. The vicar made it his business to visit regularly all the chronic sick and elderly and sometimes made referrals to social services. His wife recruited volunteers, often themselves retired, preferably car drivers, who were asked to do jobs for the elderly such as shopping, fetching prescriptions, and transporting them to and from events like bingo in the community centre. The scheme developed entirely due to the drive and energy of the vicar's wife. She organized the schools to cook lunch for the pensioners three times a week laid on at the community centre. She set up a drop in centre in the foyer of the church where tea and coffee were available in the mornings and where advice on benefits and welfare entitlements was on hand. The drop in centre was there for the use of any resident but it was predominantly the elderly who took advantage of it.

An example of a happy Omega resident was seventy nine year old Mrs. Knight, a widow who had been the first tenant some nineteen years earlier in a two storey block of flats for the elderly. Her married sons lived on the estate and her grandchildren called in to see her on their way home from school. Her sons did bits of decorating or small household repairs so that she was not entirely dependent on the council. She had lunch with her sons on a Sunday, went to the pensioners' lunch at the community centre once a week, and bought fish and chips from a mobile van two days a week. Although Mrs. Knight had a heart condition and bad legs she enjoyed an active social life. Opposite her flats was a wardened block for the elderly with evening bingo and coffee mornings to which she went two or three times a week. Three evenings she went to bingo in the community centre transported there and back by 'Good Neighbours'. On Thursday afternoons also at the community centre was a pensioners' club and on her way back from this event, with her 'Good Neighbours' lift, she visited the central supermarket to do her weekly shopping. She knew about the coffee mornings on the church premises but had no free time to go. Most of her neighbours in the flats were widows like herself:

I go into Lil's every day and get something for her dinner. She's disabled and I have two cups of tea. I'm in and out.

She was also in and out and drinking tea with Elsie, Glad and Lulu. She never bothered about teenage noise late at night and she liked all the children in the area:

They're ever so friendly. They call out Hello Nellie when I'm in the street. They're never any trouble. It's a wonderful place Omega.

Thus it was evident that some of the traditional elements of 'community' had been reconstructed successfully, mainly by the efforts of the 'Good Neighbours' scheme, for the seven per cent of Omega residents who were pensioners.

But for the estate as a whole no respondent ever claimed that there was a 'community spirit' and many bemoaned the lack of it. There must be something in 'common' for 'community' to exist, and the size, heterogeneity and high tenancy turnover on Omega worked against this feeling.

This was demonstrated in the apathy shown by residents when their city councillors, aware of the frustration felt by residents at the communications gap between local authority agencies and tenants, sent round a questionnaire to every household inviting their opinions and suggestions on various possible improvements to the layout and amenities. Fewer than one in five returned the questionnaires. The improvements were duly made although by then most people had forgotten they had been consulted. Out of this idea however grew an organization called the Residents' Council which was supposed to be made up of thirty persons drawn from all parts of the estate. This council was equivalent in political standing to a parish council and aimed to directly represent the views and interests of the estate to the city council. In practice very few new residents were drawn in and the Residents' Council ended up largely composed of the same group of active organisers who already ran the community centre association and everything else as well. Respondents in the study said either that they had never heard of the Residents' Council or else that it was dominated by a ruling clique. Since few newcomers volunteered to stand, that state of affairs was inevitable. The scale was too big, the strings of power too remote, the motivation for involvement too low.

But this generalisation applied only to the estate as a whole. Among subgroups, among neighbourhoods, among those with particular interests, there flourished numerous associations which, for the people involved, certainly did engender the elusive quality of community spirit. There were too few of these associations and they usually depended, as is often the case, on the enthusiasm and dedication of one or two individuals. The 'Good Neighbours' scheme was an example. There was also an Allotments Association which pressured the council into clearing and fencing bits of wasteland for growing vegetables. There was a Rabbit Club and a Pigeon Club. There was an Adventure Playground Committee which set itself the daunting task of working through the bureaucratic procedures necessary for the various council departments to get themselves coordinated to clear wasteland, fill in a ditch, and lay the basis for a play area.

And there was one remarkable grassroots association which was fighting back against the problems endemic on the estate. It was working because the people involved had intuitively grasped what had gone wrong in the planning of Omega. The Farm End Association grew out of a successful street party in Farm End Road in Jubilee year. A forceful kindly woman called Mrs. McCreedy who had a large grownup family had helped to organise the street party and realised:

167

There were some close neighbours that met for the first time at that party. One man hadn't talked to any of his neighbours since he moved in fifteen years ago.

Mrs. McCreedy took it upon herself to circulate the three hundred or so households in Farm End Road and the streets adjoining asking them if they would pay 30p a month to join a neighbourhood association:

Within the month we had a constitution and a bank and a committee of six.

The street parties had been a catalyst in other areas of the estate too for such associations to spring up but elsewhere they became a means of organising social events like Christmas parties and summer day trips for children and nothing more. But because of Mrs. McCreedy, the Farm End Association became a smallscale personalised informal and well resourced branch of the social services. Presumably because of her personality and because she was one those people who knew everybody, Mrs. McCreedy cajoled numerous people into becoming volunteer helpers.

The Association ran a weekly tote which involved the collecting of money. The volunteers called on their neighbours and exchanged news at the same time. All the pensioners were called on in cold weather to see if any shopping needed doing and they all received a food parcel at Christmas. All new mothers and anyone bereaved received flowers and a message from the Association. Mrs. McCreedy's house was 'open door' for Association business and any callers after 6 o'clock every evening. This way she was able to learn of persons with specific needs with which the Association could help. For example several TV licences were paid for and a store of clothes left over from estate jumble sales was kept in the garage available to anyone who wanted to rumage for something needed for the children. Specific requirements for another bed, for a cooker or for a carpet were also met by the Association. This was Mrs. McCreedy's special talent. She was a regular caller to the local radio station who were always happy to give her time to broadcast a request for some item badly needed by someone. She was also well known to all the big business firms in the area. A leading garage chain had given her an out of service van which her volunteers soon got tuned up. At Christmas nearly every business gave Mrs. McCreedy something blackmailed by the threat that, if they did not, every listener to the local radio would be told of their meanness.

During the evenings Mrs. McCreedy's understanding of the system was used by callers wanting help filling in forms, advice on rent rebates, or a character reference for an impending court appearance. And the local beat policeman knew there was always a cup of tea for him. She would sometimes tell him of a local youngster causing trouble at home or suspected of stealing by his parents, knowing that he would find an opportunity to talk to the boy and warn him in a friendly informal way. In the same way she alerted the policeman if she learned that a wife was getting beaten but did not want to report her husband. Mrs.McCreedy believed in prevention, tolerance, informality, containment and self-help.

The Association also had long term aims. The chief one of these was to get their own local neighbourhood community centre built. They got planning permission for a building on a piece of waste ground in their area, all the labour was to be provided by local men but they needed money for the materials. They applied to the council for financial support and a long bureaucratic process of procrastination began during which the estimated cost of materials went up by a factor of ten. They won through and eventually a club house began to be built which was to be used every day for mothers' and toddlers' playgroups, pensioners' drop in coffee mornings, children's holiday activities, evening youth clubs and adult socials.

It was encouraging that residents in the Farm End neighbourhood had nothing but favourable remarks to make about the Association and no-one criticised Mrs. McCreedy for meddling. Outside the neighbourhood and particularly in the community centre association there was a lot of resentment and hostility engendered by what were seen as unreasonable demands by the Association for the hiring of halls, and no doubt by jealousy at the success and popularity of the Association in its own area. One secret of this success must have been the fact that Mrs. McCreedy was very definitely not a selfrighteous do-gooder. In fact there had been a time when the McCreedys could have been categorised as rough. They had caused headaches for succeeding waves of social workers since the family had moved to Omega. The eldest son had 'done time', one of the girls had been a very wild teenager, running away from home with older men and becoming a single parent at fifteen, and Mr. McCreedy was longterm unemployed. There was thus no suspicion of Mrs. McCreedy giving herself airs since she had been through it all. Most remarkable of all however was the analysis of the root causes of the problems of Omega given by Mrs. McCreedy:

> We've a population of ten thousand and half of them are children. Yet we've one community centre and a scout hut. For children up this end, they've to walk half a mile or go through the park and there's been a lot of attacks there. We want to build something in this area we can call our own. The building is our main aim so that we can cut vandalism. If we can get the youngsters into a small local centre which they can take pride in and feel they belong.

> Omega is too big to be treated as a unity. You can't impose things from the top like this Residents' Council. People want someone they know. And first you've got to get people to know each other. So you've got to have somewhere to go, somewhere in your neighbourhood that's not too far for kids on their own, and where you know you'll know people.

> People are very suspicious of officialdom here. They feel they're the forgotton people. Dealing with the housing or with social services, it's like dealing with God, trying to get in touch with somebody at the top that can do something. You just have to persistently keep on going back to them and back again until they realise here's someone who won't go away. In the end you do win against the system. But it's not right. They're supposed to be services for the public, that's us.

The success of the Farm End Association on Omega indicated that there were resources within its population which if not continually frustrated by environmental and administrative deficiencies could operate in time to give cohesion and identity to human scale neighbourhoods within the larger estate. If that could be fostered a lot of Omega's problems would disappear.

12 Conclusions

The many aspects of life as experienced on Omega estate considered in this report lead to the identification of the following factors, each contributing to, or aggravating, or causing, problems.

SIZE AND SITUATION

Omega contained nearly three thousand households and was the largest estate in the city. There were three other estates with over a thousand dwellings and two of these were almost as unpopular and troublesome as Omega. The third was Chalkbury, compared with Omega throughout this report, and used as an example of a popular estate with few problems. There was one big difference between Chalkbury and the other three large estates. Chalkbury, although built at the same time in the fifties and sixties, was situated within the old established boundaries of the city. Moreover although it was all called Chalkbury, and it was all part of the one plan, in fact there were distinct sub-estates of two or three or four hundred dwellings divided from each other by a busy main road and hospital grounds. Each patch of housing lay adjacent to prewar owner occupied houses and streets of shops. The schools, shops and other amenities drew from a broad socially mixed population. Chalkbury was not a single identifiable geographical unity.

In contrast the others were built as one large block of council housing on the periphery of the city on green field sites. They had been provided with their own schools, public houses, community centres and shops. It was an expensive bus ride into the city centre. There was a sense of isolation and nobody ever passed through on their way to anywhere else. Since these areas were clearly defined and named, any crimes committed or trouble made for authorities were easily identified with the estate. A bad reputation once made, stuck.

The planners evidently hoped that by providing amenities the estates would become communities. But the estates were too large for that. Mrs. McCreedy knew this when she drew a notional line round the streets and drives in the Farm End Road vicinity, containing three hundred households, and determined to build a meeting hall and develop a community service for just their neighbourhood. The NACRO study (1984) of inner London estates came to a similar conclusion:

> We have found that estates of more than 800 units are often too large for their residents to readily identify with, and people seem to prefer belonging to smaller units . . . . and there seems to be an inverse correlation between the size of the estate and the number of tenants participating in any association.

NACRO went on to suggest that local authorities divide up the larger estates into smaller ones 'with separate names, boundary fences, community facilities and management'. Power (1984) of the Priority Estates Project wrote:

> Big estates make for problems . . . . Their uniformity and 'public utility' image and their usually high density can induce a feeling of segregation and underprivilege. From the council's point of view the ineffectiveness of remote management is compounded many times over by size.

In Power's study also any estate with more than 800 dwellings was considered large yet Omega had 3,000 dwellings. Enlightened council policies could encourage the emergence of identifiable neighbourhoods by supporting resident intiatives and setting up straightforward procedures for obtaining practical and financial assistance for enterprises to provide social meeting places and neighbourhood care in localised patches of housing. The appointment of a community liaison officer could help in this direction. It would be to everyone's advantage, not

172

least the local authority's, if the untapped resources within ordinary residents were released in this way.

As Coleman has stated after a national survey of land use (Inlogov 1982) there is no need for local authorities to build vast areas of public housing on what could be agricultural land, although it might be from a planner's point of view more convenient. There are patches of land within cities and within satellite towns and villages where numerous small estates could be built which would avoid all the disadvantages of Omega for the residents and allow them to contribute to city or village life.

POPULATION COMPOSITION

The extraordinary age distribution on Omega at the time of the 1961 census with half the population under sixteen and hardly anyone over forty five, was already mentioned in Chapter 7. The estate was built for families thousands of which were on the waiting list in the fifties. The men of these families were mostly factory workers. Fifty per cent of the household heads in the early days were of skilled worker category; twenty five per cent were classified as unskilled workers with twelve per cent white collar workers (the lowest proportion anywhere in the city) and thirteen per cent in the army or unclassified. Half the early settlers had come to the area from elsewhere chiefly from Scotland or Ireland attracted by the booming Midlands industries of the time.

The city sat back as the housing lists dwindled and waited for the estate to 'settle'. A local newspaper wrote in the mid-sixties:

> Omega is in a state of flux, it is unsettled, and
> the community has not had time to settle into a
> normal pattern of life.

But that was easier said than done with the bulge of child numbers gradually moving up the age scale, grossly underprovided for in terms of amenities, and with the deficiencies in design and the structure of the housing becoming apparent.

And then other processes began to work. Over the next ten years the proportion of skilled workers on Omega dropped to forty three per cent and then by 1981 to only thirty six per cent, while the unskilled rose to forty two per cent. Unemployment, negligible when the estate was built, crept to three per cent by 1971 a figure however which was lower than the five per cent for Chalkbury or the city as a whole. By the 1981 census that picture had changed. The rate on Omega was fifteen per cent compared with the city average of eleven per cent and the Chalkbury figure of twelve per cent. Two or three years later it was estimated locally at closer to twenty per cent for Omega as a whole and over fifty per cent of those aged sixteen to nineteen years on the estate. Unemployment and its resulting deprivation and demoralisation hit Omega hardest because of the huge proportion of unskilled teenagers in its population; and because of its almost total dependence on a number of factories in related industries which began contracting. Without the constant demand for workers by those industries the very basis of Omega's existence was undermined, a reminder of the shortsighted planning which brought it into being.

HOUSING ALLOCATION POLICY

There were also other changes taking place which worked towards increasing the proportion of disadvantaged families on Omega. Other indicators of social and economic disadvantage listed in Chapter 3 such as children in care, rent arrears, large families, single parents, domestic disputes, victimisation and delinquency were all worse on Omega in the 1980s than anywhere else in the city. It also had the highest percentage of West Indian immigrants.

In the 1970s there were changes made in the respective responsibilites of housing departments and social services for the homeless. Until then there was no legal obligation on the part of councils to house anyone unless they were the victims of slum clearance or compulsory purchase. There was a 'right to be rehoused' but not a 'right to housing'. Councils took applications for tenancies only from selected categories such as married couples and families. In 1977 the Housing (Homeless Persons) Act made homelessness the mandatory responsibility of the local authorities although two categories were excepted, those with 'non-priority need' (in practice the single homeless) and the intentionally homeless. In theory housing became everyone's right. The categories which could be allocated permanent tenancies widened to include single parents, unmarried couples and families evicted by private landlords. In fact slum clearance and rent controls had reduced private landlords to a diminishing species anyway. During the same period some authorities began a limited sale of council houses to the more prosperous longstanding tenants, a process accelerated in the 1980s by government legislation. Thus on a national scale the last decade has seen an increasing trend for council housing to cater for the most economically disadvantaged third of British households.

Nevertheless some, like Omega, became more disadvantaged than others, like Chalkbury, for which the answer could be found in the city housing department procedures and records. An information sheet provided to an applicant for housing by the city gave facts and figures on each of the estates administered by the city. Each estate was categorised as having 'little or no turnover', 'very few vacancies', 'occasional vacancies', 'reasonable turnover' or 'fairly regular turnover'. This was a code which told prospective tenants that if they wanted an offer in a reasonable period of time then they had better put their names down for somewhere in one of the last two categories. Chalkbury was in the first category. The three large peripheral problem estates of which Omega was one were in the last category. Most ordinary applicants nevertheless put other estates as their preference and many also wrote on the form that they would under no circumstances consider a tenancy on one of the unpopular three estates. To increase the problems of the housing department over seventy per cent of applications for a transfer were from existing tenants on those same estates. Even with a strictly fair system and the best will in the world it was inevitable that the young family evicted from rented rooms, the single mother living with her parents in an already overcrowded house, the large noisy quarrelsome family with three Alsatians pushed off a more popular estate by residents' petition, should be offered a place on Omega. Nor did the families have much choice themselves considering the urgency of their need. Up until the early seventies such families would have been placed in shortlife '1954 Act' housing (property designated for eventual demolition) a system which produced its own problems. Those areas had now been redeveloped and urgent cases had to go wherever a suitable vacancy came up at short notice. In this way the most vulnerable and the least socially competent families had a more than average probability of ending up on Omega. As long ago as 1963 Wilson in a now classic paper wrote that:

> Some concentration of socially deprived tenants is inevitable . . . . Once estates have been established for some time and begun to acquire a 'tone' and a tradition, transfers and exchanges will accelerate the process of self selection. Tenants

who want to move away from Botany Bay can only be replaced by tenants wishing or willing to move into Botany Bay, knowning its reputation.

The causal factor identified in the selfselection hypothesis was reputation. In Chapter 1 other studies were cited (Damer 1976; Gill 1977; Bottoms and Xanthos 1980; Herbert 1982) which demonstrated that problem estates could invariably trace back their bad reputations to the 'image' outsiders had of earlier types of tenants such as families from the slums or violent Celtic clans. The history of Omega as related in Chapter 2 showed that from the beginning the estate was associated with 'foreign' workers come to get rich at the factories, with large rough families, and to a lesser extent with slum clearance. It was never accepted as part of the city proper and its reputation began the downward spiral which the housing allocation system could do nothing to prevent.

THE DIVIDED PEOPLE

On all housing estates studied sociologically comment has been made on divisions bewteen 'rough' and 'respectable' families. These studies were referred to in Chapter 1. It was suggested there that conflict between types of family hostile to each other might be a more telling characteristic of problem estates than the degree of social and economic deprivation. It is worth pursuing this idea further in the light of findings from Omega.

Certainly residents on Omega divided themselves by labels. Selfstyled 'decent people' worried about their children playing with 'kids from rough families' or 'picking up rough language'; 'a welfare family' was a derogatory term as was 'a bad lot' or 'not our sort'. From the other side of the divide people complained of 'snobs', 'nosey parkers' or 'they think they own the place'. These distinctions reflected different lifestyles and had implications for the social life of the estate. As with other studies there were the respectables, families with high standards and self esteem who were disapproving of other types and were unlikely to mix socially or let their children play with roughs. The Sands, the Dales, the Sowters, the Sumners, the Lanes and many others, indeed the majority, were in the respectable category. The roughs of course were so named because their children were alleged to run wild and be foulmouthed and because their homes were often uncared for. They were also associated with being on welfare and being generally undeserving. By and large roughs were sociable but defensive like the Longs or the Donaldsons and things tended to get too much for them at times. Within the roughs however was a category of people who were indifferent or hostile to their neighbours, who did not seem to consider or care how much their behaviour upset or inconvenienced others, and who would verbally or even physically attack those who complained. These have been termed the antisocials and the Rileys and the Donaldsons' neighbours were in this category.

Omega was divided in other ways as well. There was the West Indian population; there was the Scots community and a faction of Irish Catholics; there were generational divisions with the elderly nearly all in special housing; and an increasing percentage of owner occupiers (twenty per cent in 1981) some of whom were first time buyers saving to move somewhere more upmarket. While all these divisions and differences in lifestyle existed it was mainly the resentment of the respectables against the roughs and antisocials which caused the overt conflict typical of the problem estate. As Popplestone and Paris (1979) wrote in their study of 'difficult' estates:

> What reached the department therefore was less a profile of misbehaviour, varying with incidence, than a profile of neighbourhood sensitivity, varying by levels of tolerance.

It was that neighbourhood sensitivity, that intolerance, which led to the high rate of reporting to the police, the social services and the housing department. Bringing the authorities in on their side was a weapon used by the repectables in the war against the minority of roughs who threatened their respectability and their status and who were responsible, as they saw it, for the reputation of Omega. On the other hand a lot of the harassment and vandalism could be seen as territorial aggression against the respectables by rough youth. The conflict militated against containment, cooperation and the development of any feeling of community.

If, as was argued in Chapter 5, housing departments should take some responsibility as landlords for the social equilibrium of neighbourhoods and estates under their management, then the question is what could be done to alleviate the conflict and resentment which divided people. The first question relates to concentration or dispersal. While slum clearance was going on, in the fifties, sixties and even into the seventies in some areas of Britain, it was general housing policy to grade applicants for tenancies according to observed standards of hygiene, housekeeping and social competence, and place those with the lowest scores in 'intermediate' properties in future clearance areas. As the Central Housing Advisory Committee (1955) wrote:

> A deviation from good standards is less noticeable and so less objectionable . . . . possible to place tenants in surroundings in which efforts at rehabilitation may have the best chance of success.

Rehabilitation rarely worked despite advice on budgeting and hygiene and nutrition by well meaning housing visitors and Tucker (1966) in his nationwide survey of the problems of housing estates damned the policy because those families placed in such areas had:

> no chance of creating or recovering a reasonable family life because of the kind of property they live in or the placing of it.

Byrne (1973) in a survey of interwar estates in North Shields attacked the effects of ghetto concentrations of the poorest families and put the view that sensible thinking:

> would suggest a destruction of subculture as a policy objective, in other words, dispersal rather than concentration.

The policy tide turned coinciding with the clearance of the last remaining areas of condemned housing in most cities. With the building of the postwar estates councils stopped grading applicants and instituted a single list on which points were allotted according to waiting time and housing need. This system, as we saw earlier in the chapter, unintentionally led through a process of selfselection to the decline of some estates while others aquired a sought-after image. And housing departments found that even with adequate material standards for all they had just as much trouble as before, this time because the respectable majority on problem estates resented bitterly the presence of roughs. The problem of neighbourhood incompatabilities and divisions has been addressed by a number of authors.

Popplestone and Paris (1979) point to the responsibility of housing departments:

> The problems that come to light in difficult tenant cases would be inconceivable in another housing sector. These families have been placed in the housing they occupy by a housing management

decision. Their only hope of leaving it lies through another housing management decision. Management must take responsibility for the consequences of its decisions.

Unfortunately Popplestone and Paris's ideas do not seem very practical. They suggest 'tenant-management' meetings where:

respectables and disreputables . . . . both could have a right to say what they disliked about each other, and a new set of bargaining situations could emerge out of any such dialogue.

The mind boggles at the picture of such a gathering with some of the families on Omega. But in fact they would be most unlikely to attend such meetings in the first place. Equally naive seems another idea of:

encouraging tenants to adopt a more tolerant attitude towards families with different life-styles.

These authors further argue for a return to an active policy of dispersal involving grading both estates and families so that 'difficult' families should not be placed on 'high stress' estates, but should be put instead into the best type of dwelling, those 'designed to give each family more privacy', on better estates. This would seem to be a recipe for a fury of bitterness by respectables and a barrage of complaints against the council.

The most intractable problem for a housing department is what to do with the notorious antisocial family. Most councils have no definite policy apart from doing nothing for as long as possible and then simply transferring them to wherever a vacancy crops up. The problem of evicting a problem family has been made more difficult for councils since the 1980 Housing Act which require action through the courts. By the late seventies however some councils were beginning to take responsibility for social compatibility in estate localities. Brent for example operated a management policy which aimed at initially allocating tenants to vacancies where they were likely to get along with neighbours. This implied a lot of subjective judgments on the part of the housing officers, almost a return to grading. However Brent was firmly against creating sink estates and would appear to be moving to a compromise situation where pockets or patches of similar types of tenants would occur on each estate. When even so complaints arrived at the department the officer responsible would visit complainants and the tenants complained of. The housing manager wrote (personal communication):

They make considerable efforts to find the reason why a family is acting in an antisocial manner, and encourage understanding between all parties in the problem.

If the complaints were considered justified warnings would be given to the troublesome family and if they continued to cause nuisance:

> efforts are made to transfer them to a more suitable property where less inconvenience can be caused to neighbours if the family persists in its actions.

What was encouraging about Brent's policy was not that they claimed to have all the answers but that they were not ducking the problem and were accepting that the council's duty extended beyond providing each set of applicants with a roof.

Other steps in keeping with current knowledge could be taken by housing departments towards maintaining estate stability. One would be the deliberate fostering of the development of kinship groups by allotting points to those with relatives on any particular estate. The research on Omega confirmed that tolerance and tenant satisfaction were highest among those with relatives on the estate. In fact a Parliamentary Select Committee reporting in 1977 made this official statement:

> The Government should encourage local authorities to make provision for housing young people in the areas in which they have grown up rather than adopting policies which push them to new areas . . . . thus, leaving behind a residue of older people and depriving young families of the support of their close relatives.

Another would be to allocate priority resources to raising the morale of the conflict-ridden problem estates. Wilson, the originator of the 'Botany Bay' explanation of problem estates, suggested positive discrimination as long ago as 1963:

> It is precisely in such estates, where local pride needs fostering that there should be better than average library provision, swimming baths and recreational facilities . . . . the morale of the respectable residents needs boosting on a difficult estate.

Morale can be boosted by increasing the accessibility of ordinary residents to local authority information and services by decentralising council services into estate based neighbourhood offices. This was discussed in Chapters 1 and 4 with the Department of the Environment's priority estates and Walsall given as successful examples.

THE ENVIRONMENT

Popplestone and Paris (1979) after discussing the stresses experienced by disadvantaged families on council estates made a telling point already quoted in Chapter 5:

> And yet the public sector has put up housing that makes extreme demands upon its occupiers even when it is well built. And budgetary restraints and architectural experimenting together mean that much of this housing is not well built. We owe something to the people who have to put up with such housing.

On Omega it sometimes seemed as though dwellings had been designed purposefully to increase the visibility and audibility of uncongenial persons or activities which so often aggravated the stresses of the vulnerable or the irritation of the respectable.

For example whoever designed poorly insulated ground floor flats for elderly people directly below family maisonettes, with space right up to their front windows, with the maisonette balcony overhanging their postage stamp of a back garden, with a communal dustbin area in a shed at the far end, shared by the elderly and families alike, and with a communal clothes drying area used as a playground by the children? Whoever designed deck access blocks of double maisonettes, all for families with children, and surrounded by open grassed space again right up to the windows? One family with an antisocial lifestyle, one group of teenagers racing round the grass on motorbikes, could spoil life for hundreds of other people.

Noise was a problem in all the blocks of flats on Omega and the box-like three storey blocks were amongst the worst in this respect. The trouble caused by the Rileys, their children and their dog illustrated the problem. In addition these flats were inconveniently planned in many ways calculated to make life difficult for what were often young and vulnerable families. The case of Ms. Field whose neglected daughter of two years old had several times wandered off through the front door across the grass and on to the main thoroughfare was an example. Mrs. Ewer pointed to the difficulties of even hanging out the washing since, without any boundary fence to contain her toddler, she had to strap the child in a pushchair, lug the pushchair down the stairs with the child and the washing, and then lug it all back up again.

But worst of all was the attraction these blocks of flats with their stairways and landings open to all had to children and teenagers as a gathering place. This was the factual basis underlying the 'Reign of Terror' scare sensationalised in the press. Ms. Worthy described the situation thus:

> The kids collect here and hang about the hall and passageway downstairs. They sit on the stairs blaring out music at all hours. We tried to chastise them once and about fifteen of them all gathered round and it was frightening. A bottle meant for our neighbours hit our door.

It was obvious that the long terraces of three bedroomed houses, with no solid sound insulated internal walls were a recipe for disaster. These houses were intended for and allocated to large families. Did nobody stop to think what would happen when the antisocial family with the four wild children was placed next to the vulnerable Donaldsons who had plenty of problems of their own? The flimsy fences were soon broken down, there were nights when no-one could sleep, days when Mrs. Donaldson cowered indoors lest she be spotted by her drunken and aggressive neighbour, and the morale of the whole street was very low. Only the semi-detached houses with gardens with which the estate began, provided the minimum privacy and insulation from others, which people in owner occupied housing would expect as of right. This is one reason why the older half of Omega was so much more popular, less victimised and had a higher level of friendliness among neighbours, and a greater stability of residents than the eastern half.

Certain obvious effects of design were recognised as long ago as 1953 by Kuper. He wrote:

> The architect who builds a house or who designs a site plan, who decides where the roads will and will not go, and who decides which directions the houses will face and how close they will be, also is, to a large extent, deciding the pattern of social life among the people who will live in those houses.

Kuper found for example that neighbourliness in the cul de sacs of the Coventry estate was much greater than along the roads. On Omega there was one interesting fact of relevance to Kuper's findings. While the rate of social services current contact for the estate as a whole was ten per cent of the households (from social services' records), there were highly significant differences between the rate for dwellings on the high density newer eastern corner (sixteen per cent), for those living on through roads (ten per cent) and for those living in the cul de sacs (six per cent). For people not living in the semi-detached houses nor in the cul de sacs life could be noisy and lacking in privacy. Long fast traffic roads had to be crossed to get to the playgrounds, the schools or the shops. The sand pits and paddling pools for the young children who got there were full of broken glass. There was nowhere for older children to go except the large and sometimes frightening park. The physical environment of Omega was not conducive to a pleasant peaceful family life even if you had no problems to start with.

Five factors have been identified which played a role in making Omega the most unpopular estate in the city particularly from the point of view of families. These were: its size and segregation on the city periphery; the composition of the population; the cumulative effects of the housing allocation system; the conflict between types of tenant; and the design and structure of the dwellings together with the layout of the estate as a whole. On all these counts it had a worse deal than any other estate in the city and as a result was proceeding in a downward spiral, accelerated in the early 1980s by the national increase in unemployment, and enforced reduced spending on housing, welfare and other services, a trend which hit hardest the already disadvantaged.

The above constraints set a severe limit on what could be expected of the city council in addressing the problems identified and the measures suggested for improvement. After the completion of the research however entryphone systems were installed at the entrances to blocks of flats which prevented harassment of residents and vandalism of the interiors by teenagers. Fences were built to enclose the patches of grass outside the big front windows of the ground floor maisonettes. Plans were made to tackle the problem of traffic by closing off some roads and putting humps in others. An estate based housing office was opened initially on a halftime basis to deal with repairs, rents, transfers and allocations. Mrs. McCreedy got her social centre built and thus at least one part of the estate felt it had a neighbourhood identity. A housing welfare officer was appointed but he was based in the Town Hall so it would seem the council's commitment to the responsibility for sorting out neighbour incompatibilities was less than wholehearted.

But set against the wellmeaning start that was made were enormous difficulties. With the obligation to increase council house sales and a virtual embargo on new building it was inevitable that there would be more and more desperate families likely to be placed on Omega as the only estate coming up with a vacancy thus maintaining the problem of high child density. The factories which remained continued to reduce their labour forces as they became increasingly robotised thus condemning more heads of households to redundancy and more young people to permanent unemployment. Bus services were being cut and fares were rising thus cutting Omega off to an increasing extent from city life.

In such circumstances and with such a prospect what will happen to Omega and to other estates elsewhere which are problem estates by the definition used in this report? At worst they will gradually and inexorably sink into areas of concentrated and hopeless deprivation in an ever deteriorating physical environment such as the outer estates reported on by the CES (1984). At best the understanding of the causes of problem estates and the well researched evidence as to what can be done when local authority motivation is high will be put on one side until (if ever) times change and the fair distribution of resources becomes once again a political objective. Because at root that is what it is all about.

Appendix of family case histories

THE LONGS (lax)

The Longs had three sons and a daughter between the ages of ten and fifteen. The family had come over from Ireland, lived in a rented room for a while then ten years ago been allocated their three bedroom house on the estate. Omega had been their first preference. They liked the close where they lived and the house although, with three boys in one bedroom, conditions were cramped. Mr. Long worked intermittently as a building site labourer. The family's only transport was one battered bicycle which Mr. Long had to return before Mrs. Long, who worked as an evening cleaner at a factory, could leave for work. They clearly had little money and had evidently been in rent arrears in the past. Mrs. Long seemed anxious about talking to researchers which may have been because her older children were in trouble, a fact which she did not admit to. She did however talk of the general problems with the children. The boys played on the green in the close and caused problems with broken windows and balls in gardens:

> There is one particular family we didn't like at the start. They think they own the place. They pick on our children, just ours. They're nosey.

These remarks indicated some neighbourhood disapproval of this family. The eldest boy Kenny had been truanting from school and the educational welfare officer had called:

> She told us he wasn't going to school. He was going
> out in the mornings so how could we know. She came
> three times.

A moment later she revealed that she must in fact have been aware of Kenny's non-attendance:

> He wouldn't get out of bed in the morning.

After the visits by the educational welfare officer:

> his dad got onto him and gave him a good hiding and
> he's back now.

Mr. Long was said to be 'strict' by Mrs. Long, but the impression given was that in fact he meted out punishment, often corporal, when he himself was caused trouble, rather than in support of general principles of behaviour. Another example of the erratic discipline the children were subjected to was when Kenny had stopped out all night on two occasions without telling them where he was. Mrs. Long had obviously been very worried and on the second occasion either she told Mr. Long or he found out and, in addition to the obligatory hiding, he had apparently made all the children go to bed at 9 o'clock for a whole week. Because of the wrath of Mr. Long when he sensed insubordination Mrs. Long bore the brunt of shielding the children and suffering the worry on her own. The girl Anna for example had gone through a phase of:

> you know, wanting to stay the night in other
> people's houses. I gave in once or twice to stop
> the noise but he didn't know. But now she's got an
> evening job in town, she gets tired and she's not so
> flighty.

There were no definite rules and Mrs. Long just seemed to hope for the best and lived from day to day:

> You can't stop kids getting into bad groups. You
> can't say you mustn't play with him or her. I've
> always told them, don't be influenced, go your own
> way, it's up to them.

The overall picture of the family dynamics which emerged after the two teenagers talked about their views was much the same as portrayed by Mrs. Long but extra details were filled in. Both Kenny and Anna had been in trouble at school for 'mucking about', for refusing to do detentions, and not being obedient to or cooperative with members of staff. As a result Mr. Long had been asked to go to the school to discuss matters and he had made them do their detentions by administering a good hiding at home. It was characteristic of Mr. Long to make sure he was seen to be in control of his children and on the side of law and order once he had been forced into involvement and his own pride was at stake. Nor was he having any interfering busybodies poking their noses into his business. After Kenny had been charged with criminal damage and was awaiting his court appearance a woman probation officer or social worker arrived at the house, presumably to assess the home background, and possibly to offer supportive activities to the children, since the youngest boy had also been involved in the offences but was too young for criminal proceedings. According to Kenny she was 'seen off' by Mr. Long, who had been drinking, with some style. However Mr. Long then administered another hiding to Kenny and confined him to the house. Kenny only fourteen at the time had to pay off his £100 fine bit by bit himself by getting a part time job. The same pattern was followed when Anna soon after was charged and convicted of causing actual bodily harm after beating up another girl. She was punished, kept indoors for a month, and again had to pay her £135 fine by getting the part time evening job to which her mother had referred. Mrs. Long had apparently attended these court appearances but Mr. Long had not felt it worth losing a day's pay over it. Neither of these two teenagers seemed to have anything constructive to do with their leisure time and both were unsupervised in the sense that their parents were unlikely to know where they were. Anna said she and her friends just 'mucked about' in the park, while Kenny tended to frequent the youth club and, after he left school and got a job, the city centre pubs. In summary then the Long family had a warm mother who tended to stand as a buffer between the erratic disciplining of Mr. Long and the misdemeanours of the children; she was unable to control them herself and felt helpless in the face of fate and the powers that be. Mr. Long on the other hand exercised no supervision and appeared to take little interest in what his children did unless their activities landed trouble on his plate at which point he felt his status threatened and applied heavyhanded retribution.

THE CLAPPER FAMILY (strict)

The most extreme case of a morally united family was that of the Clappers, a West Indian family with eight children between six and twenty, who had lived on the estate eighteen years. They were Seventh Day Adventists and their life revolved around their church. They could have lived anywhere. Their house was in a small close on the edge of the estate and they did not know any other parts of the estate at all. They felt their neighbours were friendly but because the family was always involved in their church work they had very little contact with them, 'just saying hello as we're coming and going'. They were teetotal so never frequented, or ever had done, the pubs or community centre. The children's only contact with the estate was at the schools but even here they seemed to live a life apart. The three eldest had passed 'O' levels, two had gone on to colleges and the seventeen year old was studying for three 'A' levels. The sixteen year old was coming up to 'O' levels. The parents were supportive of the schools, visited on open days and Mrs. Clapper said:

> I hope I'm not talking too soon but we've never had any bother that I hear everyone talking about. I think it's the good Christian background and I'm always at home for them.

The children never went to any clubs or activities on the estate whatsoever:

> We have our own youth club, wouldn't use the ones on the estate. There's a special young people's group and it's very active. We have our own missionary work and community work and there's the welfare band. There was a trip to France last summer and they went to Wales two weeks ago (half term). There's plenty of entertainments outside the home with our church, there's so much for them to do there's not enough time to do it all. They don't have time to mix with other children round here because they're fully occupied.

The Clappers did not seem to have laid down rules as did many of the other strict households:

> They just followed the general pattern. We wouldn't allow them to keep company with children who isn't well behaved. They don't go out unsupervised. The rule is there but I've never had to enforce it, they don't want to do these things anyway. All their time is busily filled with church activities. They just got started off on the right footing when they was small.

As if this was not enough the family had homecentred activities too.

> All four girls are good at the piano and the boys play the guitar and the violin. I do sewing for

people and the girls all sew and knit all the time.

There was no TV set. One can only reel with admiration at this upright united family. The temptations and distractions of the teenage life of Omega were bad enough for any family with children growing up but in this case there was the additional factor of the proximity of a substantial number of West Indian families of a different kind, with a free and easy, partyloving lifestyle and 'Rasta' children. Mrs. Clapper did express a worry, however over sixteen year old Harry:

> He's our biggest problem. He goes and watches TV at his friend's nearby.

THE JORDAN FAMILY (lax)

The Jordan parents appeared to be a very warm and sociable couple. They both had numerous sisters and brothers living on the estate. In fact Mr. Jordan's family had been one of the earliest to move onto Omega. They had plenty of contact with their neighbours, got on well with their black nextdoor neighbours (although they disapproved of 'coons' in general) and tended to invite people back from the pub on Saturday nights for which purpose they had acquired on the HP a wellstocked bar for their sitting room. They both had fulltime jobs as did the two oldest children, a girl of eighteen and a boy of twenty, in addition to which Mr. Jordan had an extra job of taxi driving weekends and evenings. Their relative affluence might well have been fairly recent because the bar was apparently still a great novelty and something they took a delight in showing to their friends and relatives. The Jordans still showed in their lifestyle many of the features of the oldstyle closeknit working class urban communities where they had spent their childhoods. They both frankly admitted that Mr. Jordan used to hit Mrs. Jordan because:

> she wouldn't keep her big mouth shut and it was for her own good.

They did not perceive Omega as a threatening or undesirable environment; in their opinion its bad reputation was the result of all the black people there. This background to the Jordan family is given because their case suggested that it was not only the stressed or particularly disadvantaged families who had a lax or unworried attitude to childrearing; this family had no social aspirations, did not want to buy a house, spent their money enthusiastically and were not anxious to maintain a respectable image or distance

189

themselves from the rougher elements, except that is, for the blacks. The children had been left very much to their own devices and their misdemeanours accepted as part of life. Their younger son's truancy from school was put down to his disappointment at not getting a place at the old grammar school and on the lack of discipline at the estate school:

> He didn't get the discipline he needed, he skived all the time, nothing we could do.

Michael at sixteen used none of the youth facilities on the estate but:

> he goes to the dogs and the horses and all the things he shouldn't. He's always gone his own way.

Michael had had brushes with the law mainly related to underage driving and 'borrowing' motor cycles. Mrs. Jordan's attitude to teenage troublemaking was evidently rooted in the way they did things in the old days:

> Years ago you never heard about all the kids coming up in court for silly little offences; they used to get a ticking off, now they get taken to court. The cops today are just out for as many bookings as they can to get promotion. Everyone thinks that things are so much worse now than in the old days but of course it was just the same, it was just that it was hushed up more.

The Jordan's easy going attitude to their children, particularly Michael was illustrated by Mrs. Jordan's comment:

> Michael usually goes into town to the pub or the dogs, not on the estate very much and then he's always forgetting his key and knocking me up at midnight or later and Dad can't hear him so I have to get up.

Mrs. Jordan said she never worried about where the older boy was and 'wouldn't ask' and that her daughter was always out with her boyfriend.

THE DALE FAMILY (strict)

Mr. and Mrs. Dale appeared to rule with an iron hand. They had six children including a baby, a boy of nine, a boy of twelve and girls of thirteen and fourteen. There was also a twenty four year old son from Mr. Dale's first marriage who was unemployed, never spoke, who watched TV all day long and not surprisingly 'had never been in any trouble'. Mrs. Dale had an evening cleaning job and Mr. Dale had been a driver for a local firm but had accepted voluntary redundancy at age fifty five. Mr. Dale was an enterprising community-orientated resident. He was organising the conversion of some waste ground into allotments, he knew the councillors, he was constantly decorating or doing the garden, and he was the sort who stood up for his rights in all circumstances, not aggressively, but because he was a self respecting citizen. Mrs. Dale said she herself had been brought up strictly and she was glad Mr. Dale was strict with the kids. There were definite rules. The children had to be in by dusk or after ten at the latest on summer nights. They were not allowed near the central shops, the community centre or youth club or the pubs. There was one exception to this rule. If the family wanted a take-away meal then the two oldest girls could go to the fish and chip shop or the Chinese provided they went together and took with them the family Alsatian dog. The Dales were very damning of parents who went out to work leaving their children unsupervised:

Next door have got kids of eleven, fourteen and fifteen. They used both to be out at work all day and the kids ran wild. We used to have eggs thrown all over our walls. People complained but the mother never took any notice, never spoke. Then she lost her job and began to realise what they were like, what they'd been doing. She nearly killed them and there's been no trouble since.

The Dales had a policy of nipping trouble in the bud. Mr. Dale told how the twelve year old boy had:

got in with two troublemakers. I went to the school and I told them to keep him away. They had to put either him or the other two in a different class or he wasn't going at all. They did, and there's been no more trouble.

The nine year old boy had got:

reported for cheeking the teacher. He got his bottom warmed and he's never done it since.

The four school age children were not allowed to go to any of the school or community centre centre youth clubs or functions, but instead attended a Salvation Army youth organisation on the estate one evening a week and on Sundays where they were Salvation Army soldiers and were learning to play in the band. All the children seemed to conform in this picture of a large, happy, united family except, possibly, the thirteen year old daughter. There were signs

191

that she was going to be difficult. While the interviewer was present she was sent to bed although it was only 7 o'clock for treading on the baby and 'giving cheek'. When she had gone her mother said scathingly:

that one'd go to discos every night if she could.

It turned out that this daughter had recently stopped going to the Salvation Army and had been allowed to go to a couple of discos at her school. At one of these a friend of hers got beaten up so she was never to go again. Within the house the Dales had strict rules also, no swearing, no cheek, and a rota of chores which involved the girls in a good deal of looking after their baby brother.

THE BERRY FAMILY (lax)

The Berry family, with a girl of thirteen and a boy of nine, had so far not had any real trouble. Mrs. Berry had faith that her children were 'quite sensible'. But even she said:

We've been lucky so far. Mine know if they got into trouble there'd be trouble from me.

That was a similar policy to that of the Long family namely, cure rather than prevention. The signs of the non-supervising and evidently non-worrying family were there:

They both do judo and gym, and Marie goes to a youth club as well but I don't know which one.

Mrs. Berry expressed her policy regarding her thirteen year old daughter as follows:

I try to be realistic, not oldfashioned. I don't bother what time they're in. They tell me what they're doing rather than me asking. I'm not strict about times with Marie, of course Andrew's younger so he does have to be in for tea, and he doesn't usually go out after tea, in the winter anyway. They're both allowed into town now. Marie's very strongwilled, always looking for the latest fashion. She got into a right state on Saturday when she wanted a new pair of jeans and I said no. There'll be more trouble I feel because she always wants new clothes and she's not always going to get it.

Marie was out of the house seven nights a week but her parents did not worry because:

she's usually at one of her friends' houses.

Marie said that if she deliberately did something her parents had told her not to:

> I'd probably get told off. They wouldn't stop my pocket money. My dad hasn't hit me for two years now.

Marie was expected however to do the washing up if she was in and it was her job to feed the dog and the fishes.

THE SANDS FAMILY (strict)

The Sands were an example of a type of family which manifested what is usually regarded as a middleclass phenomenon, that of making sure their children were fully occupied in constructive activities involving the learning and practice of skills. In the Sands' case, their daughter of seven was a much cherished 'late baby' whose older sisters and brothers were grown up, and to whom the parents clearly devoted a lot of time. Thus Sally went to a swimming club on Mondays and Saturdays, practised in a church choir on Wednesdays and Sundays, went to brownies on Tuesdays, and tap dancing on Thursdays, and ballet on Sunday mornings. Her mother took her everywhere, stayed and watched, and brought her back. Sally was also one of the children sent as a deliberate policy to the Roman Catholic primary school although the Sands were not themselves Catholics. The grownup children, whose schooling had been prior to the introduction of the comprehensive system, had passed the eleven plus and gone to grammar schools in the city. That there was an element of deliberate policy in Sally's fulltime participation in organised activities, and that it was not only a matter of social aspirations for her, was suggested by some comments made by Mrs. Sands concerning her older children:

> We had no problems with Stephen. We encouraged him to join the Territorial Army and that kept him out of mischief, then he went into the Forces at seventeen. And Kim, well I don't think things were as dangerous for a girl then as they are now, but she went to guides and rangers and if she went anywhere else she always phoned and Dad picked her up in the car.

MS. ANDREWS (lax)

Ms. Andrews was divorced and had brought up two grownup daughters and a sixteen year old son. The impression was

that she had found it difficult to cope with her son's
adolescence and, for whatever reason (she had a full-time
job for one thing), had become resigned to the fact that he
would do what he wanted regardless. So while Ms. Andrews
and her remaining daughter rarely went out of an evening
believing the estate too dangerous Gary went where he liked
and his mother would not know where he was:

> He just hangs about, that's all, or goes to his
> mates' houses. I like to know who he's with and
> where he's going but he doesn't answer. He roams
> about.

Gary had been in trouble both at school and with the police
but Ms. Andrews evidently felt there was no way she could do
anything about it. He had been truanting:

> They talked to him and so did I, it was a lady. He
> has lapses. He goes for a bit then skives off
> again. He's just putting in his time till Easter
> when he can leave. He goes when he feels like it,
> not much I can do about it.

He had also been in trouble over underage driving of
motorcycles:

> He gets bored, he got involved with a gang out of
> boredom. Then they get up to mischief. He tends to
> be easily led. They need more organised things for
> them, discos and weekends away for teenagers.

The only rule that Ms. Andrews imposed and kept to was that
Gary could not have more than one friend in the house
although they could congregate in the garden. This rule of
course meant that he spent more time outside on the street.
In Ms. Andrews' case the indication was that she would have
been more supervising and controlling of her son if it had
been a practical possibility but with no father to share the
responsibility there was little she could do to impose rules
against his will and she wanted to maintain a good
relationship with him.

THE RHODES (strict)

Though the Rhodes have been included in the strict category
the strictness in their case did not seem to involve so much
the imposition of discipline and rules as an involvement in
and caring about the children's activities and whereabouts.
But this involvement implied a strong measure of supervision
and thus merited inclusion in the category. The Rhodes had
five children between nine and sixteen. Mr. Rhodes had been

a skilled worker at a factory but had been made redundant.
Mrs. Rhodes had a part time job. As Mr. Rhodes said:

> Moneywise we could really do with the wife working
> fulltime but we wanted the kids always to have
> someone to come home to, always to know that one of
> us was here if they needed us. There's a lack of
> parental care, and I don't mean control, I mean
> care, in general nowadays and on estates in
> particular. We like them in as it's getting dark,
> we don't like them out after dark. The older ones
> are allowed into town, they're old enough now.

There was no question in the Rhodes' case of feeling
threatened by the environment of the estate, no question
either of actively dissociating themselves from the rougher
elements. Thus the children all went to local schools and
local youth club. What marked the Rhodes off from the lax
and unworried parents was their supportive care and interest
in their children. For example with four children still at
school the Rhodes visited the schools to see teachers and
work:

> every time, we never miss if we can help it.

Mrs. Rhodes had a number of relatives on the estate and:

> their nan makes tea and biscuits if they call in
> there on their way home from school.

Mrs. Rhodes was also very neighbourly:

> in and out of houses all the time, every day.

They were all very happy living in their part of the estate
as Mr. Rhodes said:

> We've no complaints, round here they're a pretty
> good lot, and the teenagers aren't bad at all. It
> all boils down to how much interest you're prepared
> to put into it as parents.

Another policy encouraged by the Rhodes was for the children
to get part time jobs to save up independently for things
they wanted. All except the nine year old did in fact earn
money this way. However the two elder boys of sixteen and
fourteen had recently had a skirmish with police for
motorbike scrambling on some waste ground. Mr. Rhodes was
taking the matter up on behalf of his sons. He himself had
actually complained to the police about scramblers on waste
ground near the Rhodes' house but had then been told that
the police could do nothing about it. He felt the recent
episode was unfair and was intending to visit the police
station that week. He had also made it clear to the boys

that any fines they incurred would have to be paid by them. Nonetheless he supported the police:

> its's good if kids get to know coppers as individuals.

Bibliography

Alderson, J. (1979) <u>Policing Freedom</u>, MacDonald and Evans, Plymouth.

Amos, F. (1970) <u>Social Malaise in Liverpool</u>, City Planning Department, Liverpool Corporation.

Armstrong, G. and Wilson, M. (1973) 'City politics and deviancy amplification' in Taylor, I. and Taylor, L. (eds.), <u>Politics and Deviance</u>, Penguin.

Bagot, J.H. (1941) <u>Juvenile Delinquency</u>, Cape.

Baldwin, J. and Bottoms, A. (1976) <u>The Urban Criminal</u>, Tavistock.

Becker, H. (1963) <u>Outsiders: Studies in the Sociology of Deviance</u> Free Press NY.

Bottoms, A. and Xanthos, P. (1981) 'Housing policy and crime in the British public sector' in Brantingham, P. (ed), <u>Urban Crime and Environmental Criminology</u>, Sage Publications.

Bright, J. and Petterson, G. (1984) The Safe Neighbourhood Unit NACRO.

Buttimer, A. (1976) 'Grasping the dynamics of life-world' in Annals of the Association of American Geographers, no. 66.

Byrne, D. (1973) 'Problem Families' A Housing Lumpen-Proletariat, Working Papers in Sociology, no. 5, University of Durham.

Central Housing Advisory Committee (1955) Unsatisfactory Tenants, 6th. Report, HMSO.

CES (1984) Outer Estates in Britain: Interim Report, Paper no. 23 CES Ltd.

Coleman, A. (1982) 'Land use perspectives and public policy' in Inlogov (ed), Perspectives for Planning, Inlogov, Birmingham.

Coleman, A. (1985) Utopia on Trial, Hilary Shipman.

Damer, S. (1976) 'Wine Alley: The sociology of a dreadful enclosure' in Wiles, P. (ed), The Sociology of Crime and Delinquency in Britain, vol. 2, Martin Robertson.

Davies, C. (1978) 'Crime, Police and the Courts' in New Society, 25.2.78.

Ekblom, P. and Heal, K. (1982) The Police Response to Calls from the Public, Home Office Research and Planning Unit, Paper 9.

Evans, D. (1980) Geographical Perspectives on Juvenile Delinquency, Gower.

Ferguson, T. (1952) The Young Delinquent in his Social Setting: a Glasgow Study, Oxford University Press.

Gill, O. (1977) Luke Street, MacMillan.

Hadley, R. and Hatch, S. (1981) Social Welfare and the Failure of the State, Allen and Unwin.

Hedges, A., Blaber, A. and Mostyn, B. (1980) Community Planning Project: Cunningham Road Improvement Scheme, SCPF/NACRO.

Herbert, D. (1982) The Geography of Urban Crime, Longman.

Hood, R. and Sparks, R. (1970) Key Issues in Criminology, Weidenfeld and Nicolson.

Housing Act (1980) HMSO.

Housing (Homeless Persons) Act (1977) HMSO.

Housing and Building Control Act (1984) HMSO.

Housing Research Group (1981) <u>Could Local Authorities be Better Landlords?</u> City University.

Hunter, J. (1978) 'Defensible space in practice' in <u>The Architects' Journal</u>, 11.10.78.

Jones, H. (1958) 'Approaches to an ecological study' in <u>Brit.Journal Delinquency</u>, vol. 8.

Kerr, M. (1958) <u>The People of Ship Street</u>, Routledge and Kegan Paul.

Kuper, L. (1953) <u>Living in Towns</u>, Cresset Press.

Lees, R. and Smith, G. (1975) <u>Action Research in Community Development</u>, Routledge and Kegan Paul.

Ley, D. and Cybriwsky, R. (1974) 'Urban graffiti as territorial markers', <u>Annals of the Association of American Geographers</u>, vol. 64.

Mannheim, H. (1948) <u>Juvenile Delinquency in an English Middletown</u>, Routledge and Kegan Paul.

Maule, H. (1956) 'The family: social and psychological aspects of rehousing' in <u>Advancement of Science</u>, vol. 12.

Mawby, R. (1979) <u>Policing the City</u>, Saxon House.

Mayhew, P. (1979) 'Defensible space: the current status of a crime prevention theory' in <u>The Howard Journal</u>, vol. XVIII.

Mays, J. (1963) <u>Crime and the Social Structure</u>, Faber.

Means, R. (1977) <u>Social Work and the 'Undeserving' Poor</u>, Occasional Paper, no. 37, Centre for Urban and Regional Studies, University of Birmingham.

Mitchell, G., Lupton, T., Hodges, M. and Smith, C. (1954) <u>Neighbourhood and Community</u>, Liverpool University Press.

Mogey, J. (1956) <u>Family and Neighbourhood: Two Studies in Oxford</u>, Oxford University Press.

Morris, R. and Mogey, J. (1965) <u>The Sociology of Housing: Studies at Berinsfield</u>, Routledge and Kegan Paul.

Morris, T. (1958) <u>The Criminal Area</u>, Routledge and Kegan Paul.

Moore, C. and Brown, J. (1981) <u>Community versus Crime</u>, Bedford Square Press.

Newman, O. (1972) <u>Defensible Space</u>, Macmillan, New York.

Parker, H. (1974) <u>View From the Boys</u>, David and Charles.

<u>Parliamentary Select Committee on Violence in the Family</u> (1977) First Report.

Popplestone, G. and Paris, C. (1979) <u>Managing Difficult Tenants</u>, Centre for Environmental Studies, Research Series, no. 30.

Power, A. (1981) 'How to rescue council housing', <u>New Society</u>, 4.6.81.

Power, A. (1982) <u>Priority Estates Project</u>, Dept. of the Environment.

Power, A. (1984) <u>Local Housing Management</u>, Dept. of the Environment.

Scarman Report (1981) <u>Report of an Inquiry by the Rt. Hon. the Lord Scarman, OBE: the Brixton Disorders 1981.</u> HMSO.

Seabrook, J. (1984) <u>The Idea of Neighbourhood</u>, Pluto Press.

Shaw, C. and McKay, H. (1942) <u>Juvenile Delinquency and Urban Areas</u>, Chicago.

Sparks, R., Genn, H. and Dodd, D. (1977) <u>Surveying Victims</u>, Wiley, London.

Tucker, J. (1966) <u>Honourable Estates</u>, Victor Gollancz.

West, D.J. (1982) <u>Delinquency: Its Roots, Careers and Prospects</u>, Heinemann.

Wilson, H. (1980) 'Parental supervision: a neglected aspect of delinquency' in <u>British Journal of Criminology</u>, vol. 20, no. 3.

Wilson, H. (1982) 'Delinquency and public housing: initiatives for future research' in <u>Crime and Public Housing</u>, Research and Planning Unit, Paper 6, Home Office.

Wilson, R. (1963) <u>Difficult Housing Estates</u>, Tavistock Pamphlet, no. 5.

Wilson, S. and Burbidge, M. (1978) 'An investigation of difficult-to-let housing' in <u>Housing Review</u>, July/August.

Young, M. and Wilmott, P. (1957) <u>Family and Kinship in East London</u>, Routledge and Kegan Paul.

DATE DUE

APR 30 1993 DHUW		APR 20 ENT'D	